LOVE TO BE HAPPY

*"It is my strong belief that we
and all other living beings
are on this planet
to be happy."*

"I have known Mehdi for many years. I have followed his search for the abundant life with great interest. His latest book, *Love to Be Happy*, is a record of what he has learned. It is more than a book. It is a travel guide for life. He shows us how to direct our own travels with the Happiness Index, the Happinometer, and twenty well-designed exercises to track our progress. Finally we have a book that we can all understand about life's all-important subject . . . happiness."

George Addair, Founder
Omega Vector and The Study Group

What Readers Can Learn From *Love to Be Happy*:

- The ten most effective ways to gain happiness.

- What beliefs have to do with health and happiness.

- What are the true "human" values, and why education in human values is essential.

- The two means of increasing happiness (Love and Service) that outweigh and outpace all others.

- Why linking with a loving Master is vital in learning to be happy.

- How to identify and reduce lifestyle elements that detract from happiness.

- How to apply the science of "Happinometry" and systematically gain more happiness.

- How cutting back on waste and desires automatically increases happiness.

- How to take advantage of your partnership with the Universe.

- Why increasing happiness is an environmental imperative and crucial to sustaining life on earth.

- Why a society's National Index of Happiness (NIH) is a more useful economic indicator than its Gross National Product (GNP).

Love to be Happy

The Secrets of Sustainable Joy

Mehdi N. Bahadori, Ph.D.

Blue Dolphin Publishing
1994

For further information, address
Blue Dolphin Publishing, Inc.
P.O. Box 1920, Nevada City, CA 95959
Orders: 1-800-643-0765

ISBN: 0-931892-71-6

Library of Congress Cataloging-in-Publication Data

Bahadori, Mehdi N.
    Love to be happy : the secrets of sustainable joy / Mehdi N.
    Bahadori.
        p.   cm.
    Includes biblographical references (p.   ).
    1. Happiness   I. Title.
    B187.H3B34 1994
    170'.44—dc20   93-6410
                                                                CIP

Quotations from Elliott S. Dacher, *Psychoneuroimmunology (PNI)*:
The New Mind/Body Healing Program, © 1992 Paragon House
Publishers. Reprinted with permission of Paragon House Publishers.

Cover art: "The Bird that Flies on Wings of Love and Service," by
Sharon Hartman

The weights attached to the bird on the back cover represent the following elements of misery: attachment, desire, guilt, hate, and worry.

Printed in the United States of America by
Blue Dolphin Press, Inc., Grass Valley, California

9   8   7   6   5   4   3   2   1

TABLE OF CONTENTS

May All the Beings in the World Be Happy

PREFACE

There is a saying in academia: if you want to learn something, teach it. I believe this definitely applies to me regarding this book, except that I am not teaching happiness; I am sharing my thoughts and beliefs about how to gain happiness with you.

In this book, I discuss how to acquire happiness, and I have provided exercises for the reader to practice in order to increase happiness. I do this without wishing to imply that I have mastered the art of happiness and am now advising you from a position of authority and superiority. Quite the contrary: I am striving for happiness myself, probably more than you are. I therefore invite you to read this book and to try the exercises suggested herein, remembering that these words are offered from someone whose joy and happiness is probably less than yours, and who simply wishes to share his approach and thoughts about acquiring happiness with you.

It is my strong belief that we and all other living beings are on this planet to be happy. It is also my strong belief that the implementation of the ideas suggested in this book, which are based on the teachings of the Masters and Mystics of the East, will help both me and you to attain the happiness and joy for which we are striving and which we deserve. It is also my belief that the happiness and well-being of the environment, as well as that of all other beings on Earth, depends on our attitude and approach for seeking and acquiring happiness.

Mehdi N. Bahadori
Fullerton, California
June, 1993

ACKNOWLEDGMENTS

I would like to express my gratitude to Sri Sathya Sai Baba, the Master Teacher who lives in Southern India, for showing me that, in my quest for happiness, I am like a bird needing the two wings of LOVE and SERVICE; for initiating the Education in Human Values program in Southern India, which is now being implemented by educational institutions throughout the world; and for emphasizing that *"the hands that serve are holier than the lips that pray."*

I am also thankful to Corinn Codye, who was introduced to me indirectly by Sai Baba, for her invaluable suggestions and comments on the content of this book, as well as for her editing of the manuscript; to Dr. Andy Bazar, Dean of School of the Engineering and Computer Science at California State University, Fullerton, for the provision of staff and secretarial assistance; and to Deserita Ohtomo for typing the manuscript.

1

INTRODUCTION:
IS HUMAN HAPPINESS POSSIBLE?

Happiness is the supreme good:
It is so important that all else is merely a means to its attainment.
—Aristotle, 384-322 BC

Happiness is that quality of life which everyone strives to acquire and maintain. By following a wrong direction to attain this happiness, human beings have inflicted immense pains on themselves and on the environment.

This book is about identifying the true causes of the human predicament and suggesting ideas toward solving the devastating environmental, social, and economic problems facing human-kind, and about transforming society from its present situation to a sustainable, joyous one.

Just how joyous is life on this planet, anyway? A sampling of information from the daily media provides a bleak picture: inno-cent men are shot to death in Los Angeles, Chicago, and New York; women are raped repeatedly in Bosnia; children die of hunger in Somalia; people who fight for their freedom and human rights are killed by their governments in South Africa and other places; people die from cancer caused by pesticides and other chemicals lodged in the food chain; children and old people in Mexico City and Tehran are advised not to go outside of their homes to avoid inhaling the excessive air pollution, intensified by atmospheric inversion; acid rain, ozone depletion, and global warming increase due to excessive use of hydrocarbon fuels and other chemicals; global climate patterns suffer as a result of defor-estation; and certain species of animals and plants have either become extinct due to human destruction of their habitats or are being driven by poachers to the verge of extinction.

This is but a small fraction of the news which we hear every day and which constantly occupies our minds. Many of us are concerned about these and any number of other devastating problems. Is there any way out of this predicament?

Setting aside for a moment the question of whether and how much joy can actually be experienced by humans, let us first consider the physical limitations of the Earth itself. Clearly, we cannot sustain our current levels of excessive material and energy consumption. Secondly, the Earth bears the additional burden of having to heal itself of ever-increasing air, water, soil, and thermal pollution. Add to that the number of social injustices and societal illnesses, the prospects for Earth and its people do not appear especially joyous.

Take a look around you, at the condition of your life and times. Is it joyous? Is it even worth sustaining, given the huge problems we face?

I believe that the amount of happiness on earth—true and sustainable happiness, along with the means of attaining such happiness—has a *direct* effect on the environment, the society, and the economy. As such, this book addresses both the causes of earth's problems and the solutions for its ills. It is my strong belief that we can all **be happy** and have both a **sustainable** and a **joyous society.**

Of course, governments, politicians, social theorists and aca-demicians have been addressing the problems of society for cen-turies. However, most of the solutions presented by various governments deal only with the symptoms of the problems, and not with the causes. I follow, with interest, the solutions offered, discussed, and implemented by various people, including elected officials in democratic countries, only to become frustrated by the superficial level of the actions, which do not reach the deep-rooted causes of the problems. Their suggestions are in the manner of a physician who works only to relieve symptoms rather than to remove the cause of an illness. Dictatorship societies are no better: no real solutions are provided for people's happiness or for the long-range sustaining of the environment. Most political solutions seem mainly concerned with preserving the positions of the rulers or elected officials who implement only those solutions that will carry them through the next election, please their most powerful constituents, or otherwise keep them in power.

In short, most government solutions for world problems are similar to the mopping-up operations after a flood. They address only the removal of mud, rather than the prevention of future floods.

Unless we find the real causes of existing problems and try to solve them, we will not see peace and harmony in the world, and we will certainly be heading to a point of time, in the not-so-distant future, when our planet will be so populated and so polluted that it cannot sustain life as it is today. Catastrophes, one after another, will occur and bring an equilibrium to the planet. What that equilibrium will be, no one knows for sure. But the world will not be as pleasant as it has been so far. The choice is ours; the fate of the entire world is at our hands, and that is an awesome responsibility. We can be completely complacent and continue with business as usual and do nothing effective, or work with the causes of this predicament and try to solve the problem.

I believe it is possible to avert the catastrophes that many ecologists and scientists predict. We need only to recognize the real causes of our problems, be courageous visionaries, and be willing to implement the solutions we find.

The True Causes of the Human Predicament

What are the true causes of the problems challenging human-ity today? Can we solve these problems?

By citing a long list of difficulties, I run the risk of sounding cynical and hopeless. Far from it; I have always been an optimist. I believe that we can solve the problems that humanity and all other living beings face today. I am hopeful that we can heal our planet and ourselves, that someday all beings the world over will be able to live in harmony together and experience happy, satis-fying, and fulfilling lives.

It is the purpose of this book to first explore the causes of the problems and then suggest ways and means for solving them. The hypothesis presented herein offers to solve the problems that we face today. The ideas are suitable for implementation by each individual. Once people accept these solutions, begin to imple-ment them in their lives, and see the benefits, they will then demand of their governments to follow suit.

In any scientific inquiry, the researcher who has some famili-arity with the problem makes an effort to formulate a hypothesis. The hypothesis is based on certain facts (to the researcher's belief). I have been trained in mathematics, physical sciences, and engi-neering. I have employed the same approach in my many years of research activities in the areas of thermodynamics, energy conser-vation, energy conversion, solar energy applications, and so on.

In dealing with a social problem such as happiness, I couldn't help but think of the solution in a mathematical context, and utilize my background in sciences to come up with a "formula," which is presented in Chapter 4, as a solution, or a hypothesis. My hypothesis is based on years of witnessing human suffering throughout the world, wondering why such suffering occurs, and pondering what can be done about it.

The hypothesis is based on the following premises:

1. We are here on this planet to be happy.

2. Due to our ignorance, not knowing any better, we have pursued the wrong means to acquire this happiness.

3. People are tired of the current state of world affairs, particularly of dealing merely with the symptoms rather than addressing the causes.

4. People are willing to try new methods to solve current problems and to influence their societies to do the same in order to attain true happiness.

5. New methods can be taught in broad and massive educational programs.

It is our nature to pursue happiness; in fact, all our efforts are aimed at accomplishing just that. Until now, the great majority of people have held that wealth, fame, higher social status and political power can secure happiness. I have observed many people trying to secure fame and riches in order to be happy. Often, once they reach their goals they discover that instead of being free, they are in bondage to their fame and material possessions, and no closer to happiness than when they began. On the opposite end of the spectrum of wealth and fame, I have known many poor people who are happy. Between these extremes are countless individuals I have met who have modest lifestyles, with varying levels of happiness or misery. Through such observations, I have come to believe that poverty, obscurity, wealth, fame, social status, and power have nothing to do with being joyous. Happiness depends on factors entirely other than those just mentioned. It is one of the objectives of this book to identify the elements that create happiness.

It is my strong conviction that the orientation toward securing happiness through the acquisition of wealth and fame has been responsible for most, if not all, of our problems. Because of this belief system, throughout history humans have inflicted immense social and environmental ills. Of course, we must each meet our basic bodily needs of food, health care, shelter, clothing, and so on, but the pains and excesses inflicted by humans on humanity and nature have gone beyond meeting these needs. Furthermore, affluence, while not necessarily bringing happiness, has had the adverse side-effects of: 1) over-consumption of natural resources and the devastation of the environment in the forms of air, water, land and thermal pollution; 2) over-consumption of processed food, low in fiber but high in fat and salt, with its attendant health problems of heart disease, cancer, obesity and so on; and 3) high consumption of alcohol with its serious health and social consequences. If we want to acquire sustainable happiness, we must correct our attitudes and beliefs about the means of attaining that happiness.

Now, I have been fortunate enough to have met many people who, I believe, have discovered and put into practice the attitudes that create true joy and sustainable happiness in life. These people are distinctive in that you can't help but be happy in their presence. They exude love; you see them always joyous. They have unwavering reverence, respect, and love for the environment, nature, and all beings. They are likely to live modestly, yet happily. Everything seems to work out smoothly for them. They even seem to have fewer problems with cars, home appliances, and other mechanical conveniences. What is their secret? They have realized that, while they should meet their bodily needs, they need to control (not suppress) sensory pleasures and find happiness through other means—through means that are much deeper than the physical senses. This book seeks to expose the secrets of happiness and to identify exact methods for its attainment.

With the modern tools of scientific research, education, and communication, the lifestyle and belief system of truly joyous and happy people can be brought to public attention. People can and should learn how to attain happiness. We all have a deep need to taste and experience true joy.

This book proceeds as follows: Chapter 2 shares a vision that I was given some years ago. It revealed our future world in a scene of great beauty and optimism. Chapters 3 through 5 examine the precise elements or factors which determine happiness or misery. These chapters also present methods for maximizing happiness.

Chapter 6 discusses the most important, and perhaps the most talked about, quality of humankind: LOVE. Here I emphasize the fact that *love* is the single most important quality for guaranteeing happiness. Chapter 7 presents the idea of *unconditional service* as a means of fostering *unconditional love* and ridding ourselves and society of all miseries of life. Chapter 8 considers the significance of keeping the thought of a Master in mind as an invaluable assist in developing joy and happiness. Many other factors that contribute to happiness, such as accomplishment, contentment, forgiveness, thanksgiving and the expression of gratitude, hope, optimism, recognition, and wishing well for all beings, are discussed in Chapter 9. This chapter also discusses modest living, implying cutting down on waste and placing a ceiling on desires.

Chapter 10 considers the cultivation of Human Values as a crucial need if the elements of misery are to be eliminated and if liberation is to be achieved for all beings. It emphasizes that, without the growth and practice of these essential human values, our race does not merit the name "human." These are the values of truth, righteousness, love, peace, compassion, desire to serve selflessly, and so on, which in fact define and evaluate the concept of humanness. This chapter also demonstrates a visualization/meditation procedure for linkage with a Master as a means of cultivating human values. Chapter 11 discusses the relationship between mind and body, and concludes that the presence of various elements of misery in one's life is the primary cause of many, if not all, physical illnesses. It concludes that *happiness IS the best medicine*.

A summary of steps to be taken toward **attaining happiness** and moving toward a **sustainable, joyous society** is given in Chapter 12, followed by a bibliography.

The reader will kindly note that the pronoun "I" frequently appears in this book. In places where I am sharing my own experiences, this usage is inevitable. In other places, I could have chosen voices other than the first person singular. By using "I" in such places, the intention is not to sound conceited, rather it is intended to serve as affirmations for myself, during the process of writing, and for you, I hope, as you read them. I believe that when we read sentences in the first person singular, our brain uses them indirectly as affirmations. I invite you to participate actively in the affirmation process by reading such passages aloud, if you wish.

2

A VISION OF A HAPPY WORLD

*Joy is the holy fire that keeps our purpose warm and
our intelligence aglow.*

—Helen Keller

A few years ago, while attending a seminar offered in Phoenix, Arizona, by the Omega Vector Organization, I had an opportunity to sit down in a corner of a busy hall and go inward to meditate during one of the breaks. It was not my habit to meditate daily or during the breaks of this seminar, but that day I had an urge to do so. Thus, during the morning break, I decided to sit down in a corner to meditate, despite the fact that the entire hall was very busy and noisy. Anyway, I sat for meditation and the following vision appeared:

I die and am buried. Then, I am born again, but this time into a brand new and quite unusual world. There is such peace, tranquility, harmony, and beauty in this world that it is hard for me to express in words. One feature of this world is a complete lack of crime and violence. I see no weapons or ammunition of any kind, and no military forces, lawyers, or border and custom guards anywhere. People have complete freedom to move about from one place to another without any fear or restriction. In fact, there are no borders separating countries from each other. Science and technology are

9

at their highest state of development, but are still being advanced for the well-being of humankind and the entire planet. Everything is abundant and plentiful. People need to work only 20 to 25 hours a week. With no crime and violence and with no military or law enforcement needed, this is all the work required of any one person. Amazingly, there is no need for money at all. Stores, for example, are filled with goods, but no cashiers. Staff are available to help shoppers find what they need. Medical and other services are available to people free of charge. Greed to have and acquire more than is needed, or more than others have, seems notably lacking. People everywhere have modest living standards and are conscientious not to waste anything. People spend their time outside work pursuing art, music, cultural events, and spiritual disciplines or studies. People volunteer considerable time and effort in giving love to one another, particularly to children and the elderly. Numerous research organizations are dedicated to exploring the laws of nature for the betterment of human life, eradication of disease, and so on. Absolutely no support is given to war games or weapon development. The environment is pure and clean. Nothing is wasted, and everything is reused or recycled. People take time to enjoy nature, trees, flowers, birds, and life in general. Another interesting and strange phenomenon about this visionary world is its population— only about half of today's population.

There was such peace, tranquility and bliss throughout this whole world that I simply enjoyed observing and being a part of it. I knew I was not dreaming, but observing all this in a vision during my meditation. The whole experience lasted about ten or fifteen minutes and I enjoyed experiencing this glimpse into a world that seems far-fetched and improbable from most current perspectives.

Is it at all possible that someday this vision will come true? Is it possible for humankind to drop all its arrogance and finally realize who we truly are, to live in peace and harmony with one another and with nature? Is it possible that our planet, so badly wounded by the abuses of humankind, can someday be healed and restored to its original purity and beauty?

Is it possible that someday humanity will drop its caste systems and all its ideas of separateness and superiority of one race, religion, natural origin, or place of birth and residence over the others? Is it possible that someday the only victor that prevails in the world will be peace, harmony, love, respect and reverence towards nature and all the living beings on Earth? What will it take to make this vision come true?

The answers depend on knowing and practicing the factors that determine happiness. The next chapter analyzes the elements that contribute to happiness.

3

THE TRUE ELEMENTS OF HAPPINESS

How to gain, how to keep, how to recover happiness is in fact for most men at all times the secret motive of all they do.

—William James

If you ask people what makes them happy, depending on their status and financial well-being, they will come up with different answers. The well-to-do people might say more wealth, fame, reputation, or social power. The hungry, homeless, and sick might say the elimination of those conditions. For the oppressed, it might be freedom, and for the poor, it might be more of the conveniences of modern living.

What *does* bring happiness and joy to a person? Is it what you have, where you live, with whom you live, or your state of mind that makes you happy and joyous?

Exercise 1: *Consider all the things that make you happy. Write them down, listing them in their order of importance.*

Happiness is the state of well-being and contentment. It is a state we strive for all the time. We have the right to pursue happiness, and **we are all born to be happy.** But what are the

factors that determine this happiness? Can we buy happiness, as
we buy the conveniences of our modern lifestyle? Will we be truly
happy when we become famous or powerful enough to control or
manipulate other people? Will we be happy if we live somewhere
else in the world, or if we are of a different gender, race, religion,
and so forth? If the answer to these questions is positive, then the
wealthy, famous, and powerful people in the world certainly must
be happiest, and the poor and the inconspicuous quite miserable.
However, we know that this is not true.

Numerous studies have been carried out to see if there is any
relationship between happiness and the factors mentioned above.
David G. Myers in his book, *The Pursuit of Happiness: Who is Happy
and Why* (1), makes a thorough survey of the research carried out
about happiness by researchers in the United States, Canada,
Western Europe, and a few other countries. He concludes that
there is no correlation between wealth and happiness, that
"wealth does not buy well-being." He has also discovered that
"age, gender, personal status, place of residence, race and educational level do not contribute to happiness." Dr. Myers quotes
from people who were interviewed about their happiness. They
make statements such as, "I would trade all my family's wealth for
a peaceful and loving home," or, "Money could not undo the
misery caused by my children's problems."

These are new findings, even though many people have come
to the same conclusions intuitively before they were scientifically
investigated. Still, society in general, despite these findings, continues to strive to be wealthy, famous, and socially powerful in
order to acquire happiness. In democratic societies, these people
work through the laws, while in dictatorship societies, it is often
through oppression and corruption that wealth, power, and fame
are acquired. Still, anywhere you go, you find out that economic
growth is the main goal and chief effort of all governments and
private enterprises. Governments plan either to create jobs directly, or make it possible for private enterprises or companies to
create jobs, and thus increase people's income or standard of

living. Private enterprises make every effort to increase profits and have more income. In other words, worldly activity centers around the maximization of income or wealth, believing that these will guarantee happiness.

In many places wealth brings people to power and, once in power, these people build up even more wealth (often illegally). In such countries we see changes in government brought about by *coup d'etats* and bloodshed. Again, the belief that power and wealth bring happiness is the driving force behind such actions.

In short, wealth, fame, and power are the goals that many people strive for as a means of maximizing happiness. I believe these attitudes to be wrong, and to be the main reasons for all of the human predicament.

If wealth, fame, social position and power do not secure or guarantee us any happiness, what will? What shall we do or have, and what shall we accomplish to secure happiness? It is the intention of this chapter to identify the parameters or factors that I believe truly contribute to our happiness or misery.

My Search for the Happiest People in the World

I have always been interested in knowing who are the happiest people in the world. I have not had the means of carrying out an elaborate research program to find a scientific answer to my question, but by reading about or talking with different people, and by visiting various countries, I have attempted to observe and inquire about people's happiness.

During a Swiss Air flight from Zurich, Switzerland, to Chicago, I struck up a conversation with a flight attendant who was sitting just across from me. He had finished serving dinner in my section and had sat down to rest. I took advantage of the situation and asked him a few questions that I often ask of people in various parts of the world. After a few irrelevant questions, such as how long he had been flying with Swiss Air and to which countries he had flown, I asked him what the problems in Switzerland were, and whether he thought that the Swiss were the happiest people in the world. I told him that I had always admired his country for being exceptionally organized and clean, for staying neutral during international conflicts, and for maintaining an unusually high standard of living.

The young Swiss answered my second question first. He thought the Swiss were not the happiest people in the world, despite what I thought about his country. About my first question, as to what their problems were, he answered, "Environment and relationships."

I did not have to ask him what he meant by the problem of environment. I knew that he was concerned about environmental pollution in Europe and throughout the world, which has affected his people as well as everyone else on the planet. When I asked him what he meant by relationships, he said, "I am 35 years old, married, with two young children, and I have been working for about 12 years now. It has not happened to me, but it has happened to a few of my colleagues in Swiss Air and to many families throughout my country. Young couples, often with two children, simply file for divorce, stating that they are tired of the boring life they have. The courts almost always give the custody of the children to the mothers and make the fathers pay for the children's support. The men are forced to pay about half of their salaries for this support, but are given the right to visit their children only about once a week." Our conversation ended here, as he had to tend to the needs of other passengers.

This young man indeed faced a major concern, living in constant anxiety and not knowing whether he would have to experience the same trials as many of his colleagues. Divorces have become quite prevalent around the world, particularly in industrial and wealthy countries. I believe that many problems in society stem from these broken homes, where the children experience less of the most essential ingredient and substance of life—LOVE.

After the Swiss Air attendant left me to tend to the needs of other passengers, I tried to visualize the life of a young man (Swiss, German, American, or of any other nationality) who has gone through divorce and now lives alone. I visualized him leaving his work and returning to an empty home, devoid of the people he needs to give love to and receive love from. What good is the beauty, neatness or organization of a country, or of all the wealth and material conveniences of life, if there isn't anyone for him to give love to and receive love from?

I have been fortunate to have made over one hundred trips to thirty-five countries around the world, mostly to give lectures, to present research articles, or to conduct or attend workshops at international conferences. During these trips, I made a point of visiting with conference participants and others, asking them whether they considered themselves to be the happiest people on Earth. Sometimes I wondered to myself if the people living in that country were happy at all. I talked to people from countries with various standards of living. The answer I always received, except for once, was, "Not at all happy." Each person tried to explain and clarify why, with the events taking place in his or her country, they were not the happiest people. These were all educated people, therefore they had a basic idea of what happiness is, and whether or not they were in fact happy. I knew that this approach was not scientific, nor could I, for example, present my findings at a scientific conference (and I was not after such a presentation); I was just curious about who the happiest people were.

The only positive reply I ever received by asking such a general question was in India. When I asked a young engineer in a small town near Bangalore as to which people of the world he thought were the happiest, he replied, after thinking a little bit, "I believe we Indians are."

Is it possible that the people of India, with all its poverty, are happier than, for example, Americans, Swiss, or Germans, who have such high standards of living? How can Indians, with a per capita natural resource consumption of about 1/30th of that of

Americans, be happier? Can an Indian fellow, who works very hard to barely make a living and whose entire belongings may not even be worth a dollar, truly be happier than an American millionaire who lives in a mansion and has all the conveniences that today's science and technology can provide?

I considered a similar question several years ago (prior to meeting the young fellow previously mentioned) when I was visiting India. I had just gone through the Nizam Museum in Hyderabad and was on my way back to my hotel when I saw a young woman walking ahead of me simply sit down on the sidewalk and begin to clear an area among the pebbles and other debris. I kept observing her as I continued my walk, wondering what she was up to. After she cleared the area, she simply lay down for a rest. It was getting dark, so I figured that she must have just prepared her bed for sleeping! This was the time that the American billionaire Howard Hughes was still alive. I had just read about his very peculiar and isolated lifestyle. When I saw this woman, I wondered who was happier, Howard Hughes, with all of his two billion dollars of wealth, or this woman, whose entire belongings consisted of the clothes she was wearing, which were not even worth a dollar. Comparing these two extreme cases, I concluded that she was happier. This may sound strange, but let us examine the factors that truly contribute to one's happiness or misery, and against these criteria examine whether this Indian woman or other poor people may possibly be happier than the American, Canadian, German, Swiss, or Japanese millionaires or billionaires.

Factors That Contribute to Happiness

Different people have different definitions and criteria for happiness, attributed to different factors. However, most people will agree that happiness is a state of well-being, contentment, and joy. It is the quality of life that everyone strives to acquire, and

everyone knows whether or not he or she has it. I know when I
am happy or not, and I am sure you do, too.

I would like to divide the factors or elements that contribute
to happiness into three major categories, one positive and two
negative. The positive elements directly contribute to our happiness, increasing it, whereas the negative elements contribute to
our misery, reducing happiness. For the positive category of happiness, referred to herein as the variable "J" (for *Joy*), the following
elements may be identified:

1. Love
2. Accomplishment
3. Contentment
4. Forgiveness
5. Gratitude
6. Hope
7. Optimism
8. Recognition
9. Well-wishfulness

The two negative categories of happiness, or the miseries, can
be described as physical miseries and emotional miseries. The
physical miseries (referred to as "F") consist of:

1. Hunger and Malnutrition
2. Disease and Physical Discomforts

The emotional miseries (referred to as "E"), are many. They include:

1. Anger	24. Humiliation
2. Anxiety	25. Hypocrisy
3. Arrogance	26. Impatience
4. Attachment	27. Indignation
5. Blame	28. Insecurity
6. Bitterness	29. Jealousy
7. Criticism	30. Judgment
8. Dependency	31. Loneliness
9. Depression	32. Lust
10. Deprivation	33. Malice
11. Despair	34. Obsession
12. Desire	35. Oppression
13. Dread	36. Powerlessness
14. Ego	37. Pride
15. Expectation	38. Rejection
16. Fear	39. Resentment
17. Frustration	40. Selfishness
18. Gossip	41. Slander
19. Greed	42. Stubbornness
20. Grief	43. Vengeance
21. Guilt	44. Violence
22. Hate	45. Worry
23. Hostility	46. Worthlessness

This is a very long list of elements of misery. In Chapter 4, we will use these elements in an equation. In order to have a manageable number to deal with, I have arbitrarily selected 25 of them, listed below, believing that if we can succeed in eliminating these, the remaining misery elements will be eliminated or appreciably reduced. These 25 emotional miseries are:

1. Anger	14. Impatience
2. Anxiety	15. Indignation
3. Arrogance	16. Jealousy
4. Attachment	17. Judgment
5. Desire	18. Lust
6. Expectation	19. Malice
7. Fear	20. Oppression
8. Gossip	21. Resentment
9. Greed	22. Vengeance
10. Grief	23. Violence
11. Guilt	24. Worry
12. Hate	25. Worthlessness
13. Hypocrisy	

Thus we have identified the factors, elements, conditions, or qualities which I believe determine our happiness or misery. After careful consideration of these lists, you may wish to add a few more conditions to the positive or negative elements, or to delete or replace some items with others. However, for now, let us consider these elements to be the more significant ones which contribute to our happiness and determine our well-being. The positive qualities contributing to our happiness are discussed in Chapters 6 and 9. The negative elements are self-explanatory; no additional discussion seems necessary.

Exercise 2: *Think of a few people you know, and try listing their negative and positive qualities. Are these people miserable or happy?*

To conclude this presentation of the various elements of misery and happiness, I would like to share a few cases or stories with you to show how these elements create people's joy or misery. The misery of attachment can be vividly illustrated by the story of how monkeys are captured in India.

Capturing monkeys in India. Most animals have to be captured in cage-like traps, but not monkeys. Monkeys are much too smart and agile to be captured through trapping. As primates, monkeys are biologically not too distant from the human species, and they share some of our traits. It is just these characteristics that humans, being more intelligent , can exploit to capture them.

In India (and perhaps in other places as well), people capture monkeys by setting out heavy jars with narrow enough mouths or openings that a monkey can barely push its hands through. The would-be captors then place nuts and other attractive food in the jars. The monkey reaches for and grabs a handful of goodies but, because of the narrowness of the jar mouth, cannot pull out its closed fist and run away. It is thus captured. The monkey believes someone has hold of it who won't let go. However, the monkey refuses to let go of the food in its clenched fist. If it could only let go of the nuts, or remove its "attachment" to them, the monkey could easily free itself.

Through the course of many years of listening to people, particularly women, who chose to confide their problems to me (as an unpaid counselor), I have observed that most people's problems and miseries are the result of one or more of the negative elements I presented above, most particularly attachment, desire, expectation, greed, guilt, jealously, resentment, and worry. If we could only learn to reduce and eventually eliminate these miseries, we could become light and happy individuals.

To illustrate how the positive elements work to create happiness, let me share the following stories with you. One deals with forgiveness and the other with how much we need to give love and to appreciate what we have in order to be happy.

Using forgiveness to heal a sleeping problem. This story appears in more detail in Chapter 9. Briefly, a woman who had gone through a terrible divorce and had lost custody of her children could not fall asleep, and was sick because of it. Her doctor, instead of prescribing any medication, employed a holistic approach and suggested forgiving her ex-husband as the best "medicine." It took about six months for her to reach the point of being able to forgive her ex-husband. After she did, she was able to sleep comfortably.

I am sure there are many diseases that can be cured, not just by drugs, but through a change of attitude and through reducing the negative elements of happiness listed above. Louise Hay (2) believes that all our physical illnesses have emotional roots. She identifies their connections and suggests emotional steps, mostly along the lines of reducing the misery elements and increasing the positive elements of happiness that are listed above. That is, she recommends HAPPINESS AS THE BEST MEDICINE.

Having someone to love and appreciating what we have. During March of 1993, a program called "A Time For Life" was aired on a local Los Angeles television station. A scene from this program showed a frail teen-age boy having trouble reeling in a fish that he had caught, while an older boy, urging him not to give up, reaches out to help him. The unusual part of this scene was that the young boy, from a loving family, was suffering from an incurable illness, and that the older one had been legally labeled a "menace to society" for selling drugs. He was on a temporary leave from prison. This boy, along with two other inmates of the same age, had a chance to spend a few days with three younger boys who were suffering from incurable diseases. They had gone on a boating trip to Catalina Island so they could be together, away from the care and watchful eyes of their regular guardians. It was during this short period that the older boys, who before this experience hated everybody and had never felt love for anyone, developed a sense of love and bonding with the younger boys. When it was time to depart and go back to their maximum-security prison, the older boys felt intensely happy and grateful for the experience. They said that this was the first time that they had experienced the joy of loving and caring, as well as the joy of being grateful for what they had—their health.

Thus, by increasing the positive elements of forgiveness, love, accomplishment, compassion, and gratitude—in great part through the rendering of service to others—the happiness of these people was dramatically increased.

4

APPLYING THE SCIENCE OF
HAPPINOMETRY

We are never happy for a thousand days,
a flower never blooms for a hundred.

—Chinese Proverb

In the previous chapter, we identified what I believe to be the major elements that contribute to our happiness or misery. In this chapter, I would like to make an effort to somehow quantify these elements so that we can arrive at a number that describes our state of well-being at any given time. Obviously, the positive and negative factors identified above may not carry the same weight. For example, while love and hope both contribute to happiness, I believe that the all-important element of love carries a much larger weight than the element of hope. Similarly, the miseries of hunger and disease surely have a much more significant effect on our well-being than anger and attachment. To show their relative importance, we need to quantify or assign numbers to these qualities of life. In other words, we need a "HAPPINOMETER."

Using a Happinometer to Evaluate or Quantify Happiness

We can write the following simple equation to include all the factors which were identified in Chapter 3 as contributing to or detracting from happiness:

Happiness (H) equals the Positive Happiness Elements (J),
minus the Physical Miseries (F),
minus the Emotional Miseries (E), or:

$$H = J - F - E.$$

Everyone is familiar with thermometers which we use to measure our body temperature. To my knowledge, there is no instrument that measures one's happiness or miseries. It would be nice to have such a device. If there were one, everyone could use it to determine how happy or miserable he or she is for a day, or for any other given period.

While there is no instrument to measure happiness uniformly, perhaps it is possible for each of us to evaluate our own state of well-being through what I would like to call a HAPPINOMETER. This device is nothing more than the above equation.

Having an equation rather than an instrument to evaluate something, such as a property or state, is not new to science. If you have studied physics or engineering in college, you know that there is no instrument to measure the physical property called entropy. For properties such as temperature and pressure, we do have instruments, but not for entropy. However, there are equations by which we can evaluate its magnitude, or its change, in a thermodynamic process. So, here too, we can use an equation to evaluate our state of well-being.

Just as thermometers need to be calibrated to give us uniform and consistent results, our new device also needs to be calibrated. To do that, we need to specify minimum and maximum values for each category and element in the three main categories of positive happiness elements (J), negative physical elements (F), and negative emotional elements (E). These calibrations or values will indicate each element's relative importance in evaluating the state of happiness at any given time.

To accomplish this calibration, I have arbitrarily selected zero for the minimum value of all elements, with various points representing the maximum values for each element. Round numbers were chosen to make the evaluation process easier. I should add that these values, just as the parameters identified above as contributing to happiness, are based mostly on my own experience and, as such, represent my own belief. I have not completed any scientific research toward finding out what the majority of people in a society consider to be significant factors in their happiness, or what their relative merits are. You are most welcome to choose different values for these terms, values that align with your own experience, if you feel they more accurately represent the various factors' significance.

The positive elements contributing to happiness. I have chosen an arbitrary total of 100 points representing the entire category of positive happiness elements (J), to be distributed as follows:

1.	Love	70 points
2.	Accomplishment	6 points
3.	Contentment	4 points
4.	Forgiveness	4 points
5.	Gratitude	4 points
6.	Hope	4 points
7.	Optimism	3 points
8.	Recognition	3 points
9.	Well-wishfulness	2 points

The negative elements representing physical miseries. I have chosen an arbitrary total of 200 points distributed as follows:

Hunger and Malnutrition	100 points
Disease and Physical Discomforts	100 points

The negative elements representing emotional miseries. I have chosen an arbitrary total of 100 points, divided equally among all of the emotional miseries. We could assign different values to these elements and still keep their sum 100. However, to simplify our discussion, we will assume that all of the selected 25 elements in the emotional misery list contribute equally to our condition. We therefore arbitrarily assign a value of 4 to each of the following elements:

1. Anger	14. Impatience
2. Anxiety	15. Indignation
3. Arrogance	16. Jealousy
4. Attachment	17. Judgment
5. Desire	18. Lust
6. Expectation	19. Malice
7. Fear	20. Oppression
8. Gossip	21. Resentment
9. Greed	22. Vengeance
10. Grief	23. Violence
11. Guilt	24. Worry
12. Hate	25. Worthlessness
13. Hypocrisy	

The choice of 100 points for each of the physical elements of hunger and disease is based on the premise that if one is starving, very hungry, or very ill and suffering from severe pain, then most probably one will not be happy, and in fact be extremely miserable; our Happinometer must reflect that. For the extreme conditions of hunger or illness, the maximum of 100 points must be selected. On the other hand, under less severe conditions, for example, when one is not feeling well due to some irregularities or malnour-ishment, is slightly sick, or is physically uncomfortable due to cold, heat, and so on, one must choose a number between 0 and 100 to represent each element of the category F. On the other hand, a person who is well-fed and feeling healthy, and who chooses the number zero to quantify his or her hunger and disease factors, is not necessarily happy. One's relative happiness or misery values must, in that case, derive from other elements. I have heard of people who can endure severe physical pains and, because of their immense *love*, still be happy. I have not met such individuals, but I believe that such people can be found. For most people, like myself, suffering from pains or hunger is enough to make us feel miserable. Our Happinometer, the above happiness equation, reflects a negative value in such cases.

I should add here that being handicapped is not a definitive reason to be unhappy and miserable, so long as the individual does not feel any pain. In fact, as reported by Dr. Myers (1), disabled people are often as happy as able-bodied individuals.

Thus, in the Happinometry equation, the lowest possible value is -300, for a person who has scored an absolute zero (0) in positive happiness elements (J), who is terribly sick and very hungry and thus scores 200 points for F, and who has complete emotional miseries that add up to 100 points for E:

$$H = J - F - E$$
$$H = 0 - 200 - 100 = -300$$
(lowest possible Happinometry value)

On the other hand, the highest possible Happinometry value is a positive 100 points, for a person who has no physical complaints (F = 0), who is completely free of emotional miseries (E = 0), and who has a maximum of Love and the other positive elements:

$$H = J - F - E$$
$$H = 100 - 0 - 0 = 100$$
(maximum Happinometry value)

Of course, a person's Happinometry value will generally fall somewhere between the two extremes. For example, let us say that

Happinometry Table 1
Evaluation of Daily Happiness with Suggested Ranges for
All Elements Contributing to Happiness

Name _____ Date _____

SELECT A VALUE FOR EACH ITEM WITHIN THE SPECIFIED RANGE					
Add all the values you select in these two rows, and enter the result in the last column.					
LOVE (0-70) . . .	ACCOM-PLISHMENT (0-6) . . .	CONTENT-MENT (0-4) . . .	FORGIVENESS (0-4) . . .	GRATITUDE (0-4) . . .	
HOPE (0-4) . . .	OPTIMISM (0-3) . . .	RECOGNI-TION (0-3) . . .	WELL-WISHFULNESS (0-2) . . .		J= . . .
Add all the values you select in this row, and enter the result in the last column.					
HUNGER AND MALNUTRITION (0-100) . . .		DISEASE AND DISCOMFORT (0-100) . . .			F= . . .
Add all the values you select in these five rows, and enter the result in the last column.					
ANGER (0-4) . . .	ANXIETY (0-4) . . .	ARROGANCE (0-4) . . .	ATTACH-MENT (0-4) . . .	DESIRE (0-4) . . .	
EXPECTATION (0-4) . . .	FEAR (0-4) . . .	GOSSIP (0-4) . . .	GREED (0-4) . . .	GRIEF (0-4) . . .	
GUILT (0-4) . . .	HATE (0-4) . . .	HYPOCRISY (0-4) . . .	IMPATIENCE (0-4) . . .	INDIGNATION (0-4) . . .	
JEALOUSY (0-4) . . .	JUDGMENT (0-4) . . .	LUST (0-4) . . .	MALICE (0-4) . . .	OPPRESSION (0-4) . . .	E= . . .
RESENTMENT (0-4) . . .	VENGEANCE (0-4) . . .	VIOLENCE (0-4) . . .	WORRY (0-4) . . .	WORTHLESS-NESS (0-4) . . .	
Substitute for J, F, and E in the following equation, and evaluate H: $H = J - F - E$ $H = . . . - . . . - . . .$ $H = . . .$ This is your happiness index for the day.					H = . . .
Comment here on the value of H you obtained. Suggest how you can increase it for tomorrow.					

Mary, a hypothetical person, considers each of the positive happiness (J) factors and comes up with a total of 50 points for J. She is reasonably well fed and, other than a trick knee and some slight discomfort from having missed breakfast in the morning rush, enjoys general good health. She therefore assigns herself only 10 points for the illness and 5 points for the hunger values of F, for a total of 15 points for physical miseries (F). Through honest self-reflection while assigning points to each of the emotional miseries, she finds herself with a total of 45 points for E. As of the time of her evaluation, her Happinometry measurement computes to –10:

$$H = J - F - E$$
$$H = 50 - 15 - 45 = -10$$
(Mary's current Happinometry value)

Happinometry Table 1 shows all of the above terms and their selected ranges. Happinometry Table 2 is provided with blank spaces for you to select your own values for the various misery factors.

Individual Index of Happiness, or IIH

With the above values assigned to the positive and negative elements contributing to happiness, each one of us can sit down every night, just before going to bed, and complete the Happinometry Table provided. To do this, choose a number between 0 and the maximum value suggested for each element, a number which you believe best describes your condition relative to that element. For example, if today you felt good about your job, were satisfied with your work, and felt a sense of accomplishment (even though it may not have been the best you hoped for, or had experienced before), you may want to give yourself a grade of 4 (out of 6) in accomplishment. You may wish to consider other factors that contribute to the value of accomplishment. For exam-

Happinometry Table 2
Evaluation of Daily Happiness with Optional Ranges for the Elements of Misery

Name _____ Date _____

SELECT A VALUE FOR EACH ITEM WITHIN THE SPECIFIED RANGE					
Add all the values you select in these two rows, and enter the result in the last column.					
LOVE (0-70)...	ACCOM-PLISHMENT (0-6)...	CONTENT-MENT (0-4)...	FORGIVENESS (0-4)...	GRATITUDE (0-4)...	
HOPE (0-4)...	OPTIMISM (0-3)...	RECOGNI-TION (0-3)...	WELL-WISHFULNESS (0-2)...		J=...
Add all the values you select in this row, and enter the result in the last column.					
HUNGER AND MALNUTRITION (0-100)...		DISEASE AND DISCOMFORT (0-100)...			F=...
Select 25 elements of misery from the list provided in the text, or from any other source. Assign an appropriate value to each element that you have chosen and enter it inside the appropriate parentheses, keeping 100 for the total. Add all the values you select in these rows and enter the result in the last column.					
(0-..)...	(0-..)...	(0-..)...	(0-..)...	(0-..)...	
(0-..)...	(0-..)...	(0-..)...	(0-..)...	(0-..)...	
(0-..)...	(0-..)...	(0-..)...	(0-..)...	(0-..)...	E=...
(0-..)...	(0-..)...	(0-..)...	(0-..)...	(0-..)...	
(0-..)...	(0-..)...	(0-..)...	(0-..)...	(0-..)...	
Substitute for J, F, and E in the following equation, and evaluate H: $$H = J - F - E$$ $$H = ... - ... - ...$$ $$H = ...$$ This is your happiness index for the day.					H=...
Comment here on the value of H you obtained. Suggest how you can increase it for tomorrow.					

ple, feeling good about purchasing something you have always wanted and needed, making changes in your home, moving to a new place of living, or discovering, inventing, or simply learning new things, can all be considered as part of the element of accomplishment. Depending on the joy you derive from these accomplishments, you can choose a number, between 0 and 6, that best describes your feelings of accomplishment. When there is anything that gives you real joy and contentment, you may give yourself a grade 4 (out of 4) for contentment. Many activities and variables can be considered in this area and, as you begin to work with the Happinometry index over a period of time, you will undoubtedly discover many activities that give you satisfaction (or misery) of which you had not previously been fully appreciative or aware. Grading yourself in the values will become relatively easy after a while. Similarly, if there are still people in your life whom you need to forgive, but you did not do so today, you must give yourself a grade 0 for forgiveness.

On the negative side of happiness, the emotional miseries (E), if you did not feel angry, jealous, or guilty, and did not worry about how events in your life are going to shape up, give yourself zero for each of these terms. On the other hand, if you had a chance to visit a friend and gossip (as we all love to do) about somebody or something (for example, talking about how bad everything is in our society today, without planning to take any action to correct it), then you can give yourself a grade 4 for gossip.

Exercise 3: *If the Happinometry Table as I have outlined it does not satisfy your belief as to which elements contribute to happiness, make a table of your own. However, if you disagree only with the emotional misery elements or the values I have arbitrarily assigned to these terms, you can use Table 2.*

Try going through Table 1 or Table 2, considering each of the elements in the table. Find out how you felt or behaved today with respect to that particular factor of happiness or misery. Then

Happinometry Table 3
Evaluation of Daily Happiness with Suggested Ranges
for All Elements Contributing to Happiness,
Completed for Mrs. M.A. as an Example

SELECT A VALUE FOR EACH ITEM WITHIN THE SPECIFIED RANGE					
Add all the values you select in these two rows, and enter the result in the last column.					
LOVE (0-70) 30	ACCOM-PLISHMENT (0-6) 2	CONTENT-MENT (0-4) 0	FORGIVENESS (0-4) 0	GRATITUDE (0-4) 2	
HOPE (0-4) 2	OPTIMISM (0-3) 2	RECOGNITION (0-3) 0	WELL-WISHFULNESS (0-2) 2		J= 40
Add all the values you select in this row, and enter the result in the last column.					
HUNGER AND MALNUTRITION (0-100) 0	DISEASE AND DISCOMFORT (0-100) 50				F= 50
Add all the values you select in these five rows, and enter the result in the last column.					
ANGER (0-4) 2	ANXIETY (0-4) 3	ARROGANCE (0-4) 3	ATTACHMENT (0-4) 2	DESIRE (0-4) 1	
EXPECTA-TION (0-4) 3	FEAR (0-4) 2	GOSSIP (0-4) 3	GREED (0-4) 0	GRIEF (0-4) 1	
GUILT (0-4) 4	HATE (0-4) 0	HYPOCRISY (0-4) 0	IMPATIENCE (0-4) 1	INDIGNATION (0-4) 0	
JEALOUSY (0-4) 0	JUDGMENT (0-4) 1	LUST (0-4) 0	MALICE (0-4) 0	OPPRESSION (0-4) 0	E= 32
RESENT-MENT (0-4) 0	VENGEANCE (0-4) 0	VIOLENCE (0-4) 0	WORRY (0-4) 3	WORTHLESS-NESS (0-4) 3	
Substitute for J, F, and E in the following equation, and evaluate H: $$H = J - F - E$$ $$H = 40 - 50 - 32$$ $$H = -42$$ This is Mrs. M.A.'s happiness index for the day.					H = -42

Comments on how Mrs. M.A. may increase her happiness index:

1. Develop a positive attitude toward the treatment of illness.
2. Join a voluntary service organization to fill free time.
3. Concentrate on the positive aspects of life.
4. Make every effort to drop feelings of guilt and worthlessness.

choose a number (from the suggested range) that best describes your condition, and write it in the place provided. Then move to the next item and do the same thing. Lastly, perform the little arithmetic asked for in the table, in order to evaluate J, F, E and, finally, H. Or, if you do not prefer to use the table, and you, or a member of your family is a computer whiz, you can develop a menu-driven computer program of your own to do the arithmetic for you and keep a good record of your daily evaluations. However, you will still need to sit down in front of the terminal every night, evaluate each of the positive and negative elements of happiness, and input them into the computer. Just like the name I chose for the table, you can call this program your own Happinometry Computer Program.

An advantage of using the Happinometry Table is the ability to appraise our behavior every day. If, for example, for one day the sum of all these elements, or H, became a positive number, we could then say that during that particular day, we were happy. If it were negative, we might say that we were miserable or unhappy. By comparing our daily values obtained for H over a period of time, we can then decide how happy we have been during that period. We can take a good look at the numbers we have given ourselves to see if there is any particular area that we need to change. Then we can start doing what is needed to increase H, our happiness. A few suggestions as to how to increase H are made in Chapters 10 and 11.

If we did this evaluation every day of our lives, we could then add up the results and arrive at weekly, monthly, yearly or even life-time values. I would like to call the annual value of each person's happiness, determined from the above equation, the Individual Index of Happiness, or IIH.

Examples. To show how one can go about filling out a Happinometry Table, I would like to complete this table for two ladies, Mrs. M.A., who often shares her thoughts and feelings with me, and Mrs. A.B., who is a distant relative.

Happinometry Table 4
Evaluation of Daily Happiness with Suggested Ranges for All Elements Contributing to Happiness, Completed for Mrs. A.B. as an Example

SELECT A VALUE FOR EACH ITEM WITHIN THE SPECIFIED RANGE					
Add all the values you select in these two rows, and enter the result in the last column.					
LOVE (0-70) 60	ACCOM-PLISHMENT (0-6) 4	CONTENT-MENT (0-4) 4	FORGIVENESS (0-4) 4	GRATITUDE (0-4) 4	
HOPE (0-4) 3	OPTIMISM (0-3) 3	RECOGNITION (0-3) 3	WELL-WISHFULNESS (0-2) 2		J = 87
Add all the values you select in this row, and enter the result in the last column.					
HUNGER AND MALNUTRITION (0-100) 0		DISEASE AND DISCOMFORT (0-100) 10			F = 10
Add all the values you select in these five rows, and enter the result in the last column.					
ANGER (0-4) 0	ANXIETY (0-4) 0	ARROGANCE (0-4) 0	ATTACHMENT (0-4) 1	DESIRE (0-4) 2	
EXPECTA-TION (0-4) 0	FEAR (0-4) 0	GOSSIP (0-4) 0	GREED (0-4) 0	GRIEF (0-4) 1	
GUILT (0-4) 0	HATE (0-4) 0	HYPOCRISY (0-4) 0	IMPATIENCE (0-4) 1	INDIGNATION (0-4) 0	
JEALOUSY (0-4) 1	JUDGMENT (0-4) 1	LUST (0-4) 0	MALICE (0-4) 0	OPPRESSION (0-4) 0	E = 8
RESENT-MENT (0-4) 0	VENGEANCE (0-4) 0	VIOLENCE (0-4) 0	WORRY (0-4) 0	WORTHLESS-NESS (0-4) 1	
Substitute for J, F, and E in the following equation, and evaluate H: $$H = J - F - E$$ $$H = 87 - 10 - 8$$ $$H = 69$$ This is Mrs. M.A.'s happiness index for the day.					H = 69
Comments on how Mrs. A.B. may increase her happiness index: Keep on loving and wishing well for all.					

Mrs. M.A. is a lady in her early forties, married to a medical doctor, and has three children. She lives very comfortably and enjoys all of today's living conveniences. She has difficulty with her husband in raising their children and often complains that "he never listens" to her. They hardly communicate with each other, except for the children's education, and her illnesses, which are due to a kidney disorder and tooth problems. She does not work outside of the home, but helps her children with their homework and other educational matters.

Based on what I know of this lady, and making a lot of guesses, I have given her the points you see in Table 3, marked Mrs. M.A. With a grade of H = −42, you see that this lady is quite an unhappy person. You may read my comments at the bottom of the table.

On the other hand, Mrs. A.B. is in her seventies, widowed, and has no children. She lives alone on her husband's pension, maintaining a very modest lifestyle. She is a very positive and loving woman, always talking about how she is so blessed to have all the things she needs. She lost the use of one arm in a stroke, but, unless you ask, she doesn't talk about it. When you ask, she says, "Well, it is true that I have lost this arm, but I am glad that my other arm is all right. I think about the one I have, not about the one I do not." She has a very warm personality and loving attitude. Because of these, relatives and friends often visit her, so that she is never alone. On weekends, these relatives get themselves invited for a pot-luck dinner, and leave the extra food for her. Mrs. A.B. is a very modest woman and never asks anyone for anything, but her relatives and friends find whatever she needs and try to bring her those things as gifts.

Whenever I visit Mrs. A.B., I can't help but become charged with her positive attitude and love for life. With what I know of this lady, and again making a lot of guesses, I have prepared Table 4, labeled Mrs. A.B. You can see from her score (+69), that she is a very happy person. There is nothing that I can recommend for this woman to do, except to wish her a long life so that people can continue to come to her, receive her love, and be charged with enthusiasm for life.

What I can suggest for Mrs. M.A. to do in order to be happy and score a higher grade in our Happinometry equation, is to change her attitude and to be more appreciative of what she has. I would suggest that she list all the positive aspects of her life and all the things she has of value, on a paper, and to go over this list often and meditate on its merits. I would also suggest that she develop faith in her future and in her physicians that her kidney disorder can be healed. Furthermore, I would suggest she join a charitable organization to fill up her free time with voluntary service, so that she can develop her love and compassion and not have so much free time to feel sorry for herself.

Exercise 4: *Tonight, before going to bed, take a few minutes and complete a copy of Happinometry Table 1 or 2, and determine how happy you have been today. To do this, choose a number (within the range suggested) that best describes your condition for each of the elements mentioned in the table. Then evaluate J, F, E and, finally, H for this day.*

Exercise 5: *If you do not agree with my identification of terms contributing to happiness (which is quite possible, and is fine with me), make up a list of your own. Identify all factors that you think are important in bringing happiness to your life. Based on the importance you place on each of these factors, assign a number to each of them, keeping the maximum values in each category similar to those suggested above. Now determine your H for today and compare it with what you found in Exercise 4.*

Annual Appraisal of Happiness

Once we have established Individual Indexes of Happiness, we can determine the major factors which have contributed to our individual happiness or misery for that year. The annual appraisal could be made during the Christmas to New Year's holidays, or preferably the week before our birthday. During these periods, we can reflect on our behavior and determine why we had the score or "grade" that we did. This is similar to students appraising their performance when they receive back their examination papers.

It is good to make an appraisal of our happiness and well-being as frequently as possible, but definitely not less frequently than once a year. On an annual basis, we can then make proper resolutions for the next year to have a higher value of IIH. Our resolutions might be, for example, to take actions, develop mental attitudes, or modify our behaviors or lifestyles in ways to give us higher points (aiming for a total of +100) in love, accomplishment, forgiveness, gratitude, and so on, and minimum points (aiming for 0) in all the negative aspects of our life. Since accomplishing all these goals may be difficult all at once, we may wish to make plans to work on a certain issue for a given month, and then move on to another one the next. As unconditional service is the surest way of increasing happiness, as discussed in chapter 7, we may wish to choose some kind of service project in which to become involved. There are literally infinite ways in which we can help others. Based on our talents and interests, we can find out what type of service is the best that we can offer; however, we must also make our service as unconditional as possible. Ideal service might be in the form of giving more love or nurturing to our spouses, children, parents, and other people in our lives. It might also be to other children and old people who have been deprived of this essential element of life. Our service project might be to help eliminate the tragedies of hunger and disease from our society. It might also be to provide financial assistance to the research foundations or charitable organizations of our choices. I am sure we will never run out of good things to do. Again, we need to determine what is the best service we can render, then do it unconditionally, with a great deal of love, enthusiasm, and graciousness.

Need to Invest in the Acquisition of Happiness

To increase our happiness, we must live in such a way that our life-time value of happiness, or the sum of all of our IIH's, becomes as high as possible. To maximize this quantity, we need to "invest" time and effort, just as we do when we choose to go on to a university to receive a higher education, or to go beyond.

Most people recognize the great financial investment required to go, for example, to medical school and become a surgeon. A person considering the medical field looks at the life-time earnings of medical doctors and concludes that, economically, it makes sense to invest so much money, time, and effort to become one. Compared with someone who simply works after high school and makes money, medical students not only forego income for all those years of studying, but actually spend much of their own money and a good part of their future incomes to get the education they want. However, to them the decision to go to medical school is economically sound. This speaks only of the financial aspects of the medical profession. I believe that a great majority of medical doctors and other health professionals choose their professions and invest time and money on them, not strictly for the financial rewards, but for the opportunity to serve more effectively. I am sure they have examined their interests and talents and have concluded that the medical profession is the field wherein they can render the greatest or the most effective service.

We need to use a similar approach to maximize our life-time happiness. Our investment is mostly in the form of spending time and making an earnest effort to increase the positive elements of our happiness while reducing the negative ones. We need to be patient for the results of our efforts to bloom and bear fruit. After all, nothing is accomplished instantly. We all learned whatever we know gradually. We received a college degree after spending four years or about 8,000 hours studying. While we were going through this training, we had the patience and faith that we would eventually reach our goals. The same thing applies to acquiring happiness. We need to have faith that we will get it and be patient for it to arrive.

I am delighted to see many people taking steps in this direction, particularly with respect to their health. For example, to have longer, healthier lives, many people now refrain from smoking, drinking, eating foods with high cholesterol, and so on. In a sense, they sacrifice some instant pleasures in favor of a life-time, or at least long-time, health.

Going back to the Happinometry equation $(H = J - F - E)$, it is clear that to increase H, we need to increase J and reduce F and E. The first step is to reduce F, or eliminate any physical problem we may have. That is, we need to be vigorous in maintaining good health. We need to learn about proper diet and nutrition, and to incorporate proper exercise in our busy work schedule, so that we can enjoy a completely healthy life.

Reduction of E, or the emotional elements of misery, may be harder than reducing F, in that it requires a change of attitude. The same thing is true for increasing J. There are many books written and seminars offered that have the primary concern of reducing E. The method employed in this book, discussed in the following chapters, is aimed at increasing J while at the same time reducing E. The chief suggestion herein is *to foster love through the rendering of unconditional service.* You will see that the actions we need to take to maximize happiness are different from the populat current strategies of maximizing income and wealth. They are also different from attempts to attain fame or secure higher political positions. I do not wish to discourage earning good money or seeking high political positions. If the unconditional service that we are engaged in brings us fame or wealth, so be it. The idea is to avoid becoming arrogant or proud because of that fame or wealth, and instead to use our status to render even more effective service. With happiness uppermost as a goal, there is no need to maintain other than a modest lifestyle while making every effort toward increasing the positive elements and reducing the negative aspects of our happiness.

National Index of Happiness, or NIH

If all the happiness values determined by the citizens of a country could be cumulated, for every day, week, month, or year, a value could be determined as to how the nation as a whole has been doing, happiness-wise. We could then determine a National Index of Happiness, or NIH, every year. This index is the algebraic sum of all the positive values (showing happiness) and negative values (showing misery) of H, determined by every citizen of the country every day, summed up to determine the annual value, then divided by the total number of people reporting their happiness values. This National Index of Happiness could then be plotted for various years to determine the happiest times of a nation.

I strongly believe that governments should make every effort to utilize the National Index of Happiness, or NIH. This approach is quite different from present economic planning methods, which are aimed at increasing individual income and maximizing the so-called gross national product, or GNP. If such action is taken by governments, we will see priorities shift, with more emphasis placed on the eradication of hunger, malnutrition, homelessness, the indignities of joblessness, and suffering due to AIDS, cancer and other diseases. After all, the presence of these problems in society contributes to the negative values of H, as reported by all the people who suffer from them. Besides, governments will surely place a great deal more emphasis on education—not simply to teach a vocation, as is done currently, but, more important, to teach human values such as integrity, courage, hope, truth, right-eousness, enthusiasm, love, peace, respect for all beings, non-violence, and the desire to serve others unconditionally. Such education is absolutely necessary in order to increase the positive values in the Happinometry equation and to reduce all the negative emotional elements of happiness.

The steps which may be taken by the society as a whole or by the government are discussed more fully in Chapters 10 and 11. Again, these activities are quite different from current strategies for increasing the GNP, or the standard of living of the society.

I believe that the quality of life of a nation in truth depends on its National Index of Happiness, or NIH. I also believe that this is a more realistic way of comparing the quality of life of different nations than by comparing their GNP's, or how much energy or material resources they use per person per year.

As you know, it is now common to consider a nation's GNP as the measure of its progress, standard of living, and prosperity. This is hugely flawed. For example, if in one country the crime rate is higher than another, all the expenditures in manufacturing and handling of guns, protection against crimes, capturing and convicting of criminals, and paying for their incarcerations add up and increase the GNP in that nation. For another country, whose crime rates are lower, with every other economic activity being equal to those of the first country, this country shows a lower GNP, and is considered less developed. The same thing is true about food and nutrition. If the people of one society are used to consuming more processed food, this consumption contributes to a higher GNP when compared to another society that consumes more natural foods (assuming, of course, that everything else is the same). The presence of many chemicals used during the food processing, and the absence of fiber and many other elements found in natural foods, contribute to many illnesses. All the costs of food processing and health care also contribute to a higher value of GNP.

With recognition of the elements that contribute to happiness, it now becomes easier to see whether, for example, an Indian fellow with a very low income and standard of living may be happier than an American, Canadian, German, or Swiss who enjoys a very high standard of living. If we adopt this evaluation of happiness, and determine the NIH values for all nations, we would have quite a different ranking of countries, a ranking not by GNP, but by NIH.

Exercise 6: *With what you know about different countries, list which ones you think are the top ten happiest nations of the world.*

5

DEVELOPING THE RIGHT ATTITUDE
FOR ACHIEVING HAPPINESS

*I have long believed the following: Everything I need to know
is revealed to me. Everything I need comes to me.
All is well in my life.*

—Louise L. Hay

Have you been around really happy people? Love emanates
from them, doesn't it? They have such a passion for life and do
everything with such enthusiasm and grace. They are energetic,
creative, sociable, decisive, optimistic, trusting, always helpful
and, interestingly enough, often very healthy. You simply enjoy
being around them and can't help but become happier in their
presence. I have had the fortune of being around a few such people.
What have they done to be in this state of joy and happiness?
What can we do to reach that state?

In Chapters 3 and 4 the elements, or factors, that determine
happiness and joy were identified, and an equation was proposed
through which we could evaluate, or quantify, our happiness. The
major elements that can bring us joy (J) are: love, accomplishment, contentment, forgiveness, gratitude, hope, optimism, recognition, and well-wishfullness, with love carrying a much more
significant weight than all the others combined. The negative
elements in the happiness equation were divided into physical (F)

and emotional (E) categories. The physical elements were hunger and disease. The emotional miseries were numerous, a complete list of which appears on page 20. In order to emphasize the significance of these terms in the happiness equation, maximum values for each element and for each category were considered. Our choice of these arbitrary numbers emphasizes that they are not equal in importance in bringing happiness or misery to our lives. While we feel happy when we accomplish something, or have hopes for a better future, the joy derived from these is not comparable to the joy of unconditional love. The happiness equation and the maximum values for physical miseries are weighted so as to show that being well-fed or healthy does not provide happiness, but being hungry or sick can wipe out any joy we may otherwise have.

With the discussions of the previous chapters and the above summary, it now becomes very easy to see what we need to do to increase our happiness: we need to increase the values of the positive elements and decrease the effects of the negative ones. (In the Happinometry equation $H = J - F - E$, to increase H, one has to increase J and reduce F and E.) This is so easy to say, and yet so difficult for an ordinary person (like myself) to accomplish. In fact the University of Life (3), an idea which I developed in a book of the same name, is established for us to increase our life-time acquisition of happiness.

Exercise 7: *Write down the names of people whom you believe have had (or are having) happy lives. Based on the Happinometry equation and the point system discussed above, try to assign these people grades that show their degree or index of happiness. Contemplate these people's lives. What did (or do) they believe in, stand for, or practice to enable them to be so happy and joyous? Would you like to have a similar life? Are you willing to invest a little time and patience to be as happy as they were (or are)? Identify the obstacles that prevent you from living like them and having the same joy and happiness in life as they did (or do). Please write down all of your ideas and thoughts for future reference.*

Exercise 8: *Certain people in history have had perfect scores (an "A" grade, or a grade of at least 90% in the Happinometry scale) for their happiness. Name a few of them. Try to get their pictures and post them where you can see them often. Keep their memories and attributes in your mind often.*

Developing a New Attitude and Belief System

Three stone masons were at work when a passer-by stopped and asked of each one the simple question, "What are you doing?"

The first replied, "Obviously, I am cutting stone."

The second replied, "My good man, I am earning a living."

The third lifted his eyes and said with a smile and great contentment, "I am building a cathedral."

All three were doing the same kind of work but their reactions were a matter of attitude. To one the task was boring, to another it was just a job, but to the third the task was thrilling. All work can become ennobling to the person who can see in it creative purpose and the importance of his own efforts.

The most important and, at the same time, the most difficult part of acquiring the happiness that we all are striving for is the adoption of a proper attitude and belief system. We need to examine our present attitudes and beliefs and, if there is a need (which most probably there is), change them and adopt new and better ones. We are all very comfortable with what we already believe in, but in order to increase our happiness, we need to examine those beliefs.

Most of us are brought up to believe that wealth, fame, position and power bring us happiness. We see the glamorous lives of the wealthy and famous on television, believing that they must be really happy. We have been taught to believe that with wealth we can buy all the things we need and then we will be happy. I believe such attitudes and concepts have been the major reasons for all of our miseries and problems in the world, now and in the past. All of these ideas were discussed in Chapter 1 and there is no need to spend more time on them here.

It is my strong conviction that to be happy and joyous, we need to develop, adopt, and foster a belief system such as the one outlined below:

1. We are living here on this planet to be happy. I accept that it is up to only me to secure the degree of happiness I desire. Further, to obtain happiness, I need to work for it, as nothing is granted to me without making an effort.

2. There are joys in life which are deeper than the physical ones. I can find out what they are, but I need to invest time and effort to acquire and experience them.

3. The Universe, with its generosity, love, grace and abundance, sustains all life forms, including mine. I accept that it has so far met my needs and, based on my thoughts and actions, it will continue to do so in the future.

4. I do not need to worry as to how the Universe is going to provide for me, but I need to have faith that it will.

5. I do not expect anything from anyone; I accept that the Universe with its grace and generosity takes care of me, as well as others.

6. It is possible to increase the generosity of the Universe, and to learn to receive even more grace from it.

7. I accept what is happening to me here and now to be the result of my own actions, thoughts, deeds and wishes that I have put out to the Universe in the past.

8. I accept what is happening to me here and now to have been provided by the Universe, and to be the best for my long-range interests and well-being.

9. I am always content, and not critical, with the results of my actions.

10. The well-being of the environment, the entire planet Earth, and all beings (particularly humans), affects my emotional state and happiness.

I will elaborate on these beliefs and attitudes in the next section of this chapter. However, before doing this, let me share the following story with you, which shows the role that faith, attitudes, and beliefs play in our physical healing process and well-being.

The commuting doctor. Several years ago I met a medical doctor who was traveling to a small town to see his patients there. When I inquired about his seemingly odd action, he disclosed the following story. He said he had been born and raised in that town. His father was a religious and community leader and was well-respected in the community. The son admired his father's work and involvement in the community's welfare so much that he decided to study theology and follow in his father's footsteps. However, one incident made him change his mind and his entire career. He fell sick and went to see a doctor. The doctor's attitude toward him was far from friendly, and the son was greatly annoyed by it. He thought that patients deserved better treatment than what he received from this doctor. This incident made him decide to become a medical doctor himself, so that he could treat his patients with respect and dignity. He entered a medical school and did very well. After finishing all his training, he decided to go back to his home town and start practicing what he had learned. He was very successful there, because, in his own words, "people knew me from my childhood, had followed all my training, had faith in me to be very knowledgeable, and trusted my diagnoses and treatments."

After a while, the doctor decided that his home town was too small for him, that he needed to move to a larger city for a richer cultural environment. He set up his practice in a large town by opening a private clinic and also by working in a government-run clinic. Then, the people of his home town came to him, begging him to come back, or at least to devote one day a week to them. They stated that they had had no luck with other doctors in town. So, he decided to commute to his home town one day each week and see patients there too.

When I asked him how he compares his curing success in the large town with successes in the small one, he answered that his success rate is much higher in his home town than in the large city. He said, "The patients who come to me in the government-operated clinic do not have any faith in me. They believe that no good doctor would come to such clinics. Therefore, my medicine has very little effect in curing them. When patients with the exact same symptoms come to my private clinic and I give them the same medicine, they get well. They believe that I am a good doctor, otherwise I wouldn't be able to maintain a practice in such a nice office in such an expensive area of town. They pay me a good fee for my visits, and get the results they want, but the success rate in my hometown is the greatest. These people, who have known me and my father for decades, believe that I am the most knowledgeable doctor in my specialty. My healing rate here is nearly 100%."

The doctor continued, "You see, I am the same doctor, prescribing the same medicine for the same symptoms to the patients coming to see me in three different places. You may think the medicine should have the same effect. Not at all. The patient's *faith and belief* in the doctor and the medicine play much more significant roles in healing him than the drug itself does."

Why is it so? How can we explain the role that *faith and belief* play in the healing process? I am not a medical doctor, nor do I know all the details of the curing or healing process. Is it possible that this "faith" and "belief system" cause the brain, and possibly other organs of the body, to produce the necessary chemicals needed to eventually cure a disorder? Does "faith" have an effect not only on our physical bodies, but also on other aspects of our lives? Another example at the end of this chapter illustrates that faith indeed does have effects in all aspects of our lives and well-being. For now, let's go back to elaborate more on the suggested best attitude and beliefs for developing happiness.

The Proposed Attitude and Belief System

The following paragraphs very briefly discuss the points raised earlier. The topics and their numbers correspond to what they were before.

1. *We are here on this planet to be happy.*

We are born to be happy, and it is our right to be so. The Universe, with its immense love, grace, and generosity is functioning to secure our happiness. The fact that there have been people who have had constant joy and bliss in life (or acquired the grade $H = 100$ in the Happinometry equation) is good enough indication to me that we are designed with the ability to reach this plateau of happiness. We are also designed with choices, and the Universe constantly provides a variety of options from which we can choose. The reason that many of us are not happy, and in fact are very miserable, is because of our belief system, and because we have gone in a wrong direction to pursue our right of happiness. Unless we change the old attitudes and adopt new ones, we will not secure the happiness which the Universe intends for us.

Left to ourselves, we automatically do the things we enjoy the most. Normally, this has to do with sense pleasures, or the things which we enjoy physically. While I do not denounce the enjoyments of the body, we need to examine our behavior and learn whether the seeking of sensory pleasures has any side effects. Particularly, we need to find out if these pleasures add to the negative elements in the happiness equation, or will make our Happinometer read a lower value in the future.

2. *There are joys in life which are deeper than the physical ones.*

We need to learn about these joys and try to acquire them. We are entities with physical, emotional, intellectual, psychic and spiritual dimensions. We need to pay attention to all of these dimensions, not just the physical one. These joys were identified in Chapter 3 under the Happiness category. They are love, accomplishment, contentment, forgiveness, gratitude, hope, optimism, recognition, and well-wishfulness. One needs to experience the joys derived from establishing these qualities within oneself in order to compare them with the joys derived through the physical senses. Many people who have tasted the joys of forgiveness and unconditional love tell me that there is no comparison between these joys and those acquired through our senses. With the little experience that I have, I can't help but agree with them wholeheartedly.

3. *The Universe, with its generosity, love, grace, and abundance sustains all lives and meets our needs.*

I accept the Universe to be magnificent, intelligent, beautiful, joyous, peaceful, orderly, living, loving, generously giving, forgiving, and ready to accommodate our needs. Depending on our thoughts and actions, the Universe accommodates us. We need to "decide, or make up our minds, as to how happy we want to be," as Abraham Lincoln said, and take appropriate actions. The Universe will take appropriate actions in return. The Universe will oblige.

The generosity of the Universe can be seen all around us, and in all of our activities and efforts. Borrowing from computer software terminology, the Universe is "people-friendly." Let us consider the following examples to see just how generous and friendly the Universe is.

Farming. A farmer prepares his land to produce, for example, a certain variety of apple. He does so with the best of his knowledge. He sows the seeds and waits. He doesn't need to do anything before the trees start bearing fruit, except perhaps water them, fight intruders such as insects or animals, or clear the orchard of weeds or anything that will reduce the trees' yield. The most essential elements needed for the growth of trees and the production of apples are provided by the Universe free of charge. They are solar radiation, water, carbon dioxide, soil nutrients, pollination by wind and insects, and all the information packed in the most marvelous way inside that tiny apple seed—the "blueprint" for the seed to grow, become an apple tree, and produce apples similar to the parent apple, rather than those of another variety. For an apple seed sown a short distance away from a pear seed, all of the natural conditions of solar radiation, rainfall, soil nutrients, and so on, are basically the same. However, there is no mistake made, and the apple seed doesn't grow into a pear tree and it doesn't start growing pears.

A *definite partnership* exists between the farmer and the Universe. If we were to quantify the values of the work done by the farmer as opposed to the contribution made by the Universe, I would give one million to the Universe's efforts for every unit of work performed by the farmer. This is how generous the Universe is, and its generosity does not apply only to farming. For every unit of work that anyone puts in to produce something, the Universe contributes a million parts.

It is interesting to note that if the farmer chooses not to put in his unit of work, that is, if he stays home and does nothing, then the Universe does not contribute its million either. It is a *partnership* of humans and Nature, or the Universe, with one million shares for the Universe for every share that a human puts in.

Another sign of the Universe's great generosity is that it doesn't want its share of the profits from what is produced. This is how it is, an unconditionally giving and loving Universe. Shouldn't the farmer feel obligated to share at least a portion of the yield with his *Partner*, say 10% of it? Of course, the senior Partner doesn't need any of its junior partner's contribution. But it is only right for the farmer to do "right" and meet his obligations. Give that share to those who are in need, no matter where they live, what the color of their skin, or what their belief system, language, and other characteristics may be. It is fascinating to note that, once the farmer does give this share of the senior Partner's to those in need, the Universe, again out of its generosity, will grant joy and happiness to the farmer. What a fantastic deal the farmer has with the Universe!

Another sign of the generosity of the Universe is that it has absorbed a great deal of abuse that humans, due to ignorance, have inflicted upon it. But it has forgiven us our abuses, and has continued to provide for us unconditionally, just like a loving mother would. No wonder we refer to it as our Mother Nature.

Flying. There are many other examples which show how the Universe has been overgenerous in helping us to reach our goals. As another example, let us consider flying from one city to another.

You decide to fly, say, from Los Angeles to Chicago. You call your travel agent and inform her of your plan. She makes a search through her computer and gets back to you with your itinerary. You pay her, pick up your ticket, drive your car, or ride a bus or a car, to the airport on the day intended, check in, and finally board the plane, spend a few short hours in the air and reach your destination. Think about all you have done. Look at the entire system that has worked to make your trip a simple and pleasant one. Look at the design and operation of the airplane, the automobile and the road, the computer, the telephone, the comfort of your home or your office to make the arrangement, and everything else. I believe the entire fund of knowledge that humankind has secured in over two million years of tenure on this planet is responsible for bringing about your flight. The fact that there are laws of nature, and the fact that humans have been given the ability, or are born with the capability, to learn these laws and make use of them, and the fact that materials are available on the planet Earth for human use, are indications of the Universe's generosity. All the things we have and enjoy today are, to me, but signs of the generosity of our beautiful Universe, or Nature.

I do not know about you, but thinking about these fascinating aspects of our Universe, and expressing some kind of gratitude to the Universe for being the way it is, gives me great joy. I guess this, too, is a law of nature—that the more we think about the functioning of the Universe and its elements, the more we express our gratitude toward it, and the more we revere, respect, honor, and love Nature, the more we enjoy our lives—and the happier we become. Remember that LOVE is the greatest element for bringing us happiness. What a beautiful and fantastic Universe we live in, and what a great opportunity we have to express our unconditional love and respect to it and be happy!

Again, in the above example, the Universe has provided and contributed generously for you to fly from one place to another. The interesting thing is that this generosity was granted only after you took the necessary steps, and did your share of work. If you had not taken the necessary steps, you would not have been able to accomplish what you wanted. The Universe would have stayed completely oblivious to your intentions. You first had a thought and a wish, took the necessary action to fulfill your desires, and then the Universe accommodated you in the most generous way. How would you rate this *partnership* and *cooperation* between the Universe and yourself? I would still give it one million to one.

We can go on and on about many other examples which show us how the Universe abundantly and generously helps and provides for us to accomplish what we want, reach our goals, and make our wishes come true.

Exercise 9: *Consider one of your most important accomplishments. Write down the role you played and attempt to list ways the Universe contributed its share in bringing about that triumph.*

---

4. *I do not need to worry as to how the Universe is going to provide for me, but I need to have faith that it will.*

We need only plan and work as effectively as possible to accomplish what we want, trusting and having faith that the Universe—our senior Partner in the enterprise system called Life, organizes and does its best. With a great deal of grace and efficiency it makes things happen.

This is similar to entering a dark room and turning on a light switch. To have light in the room we do not need to worry about, or even know, where the energy comes from. The utility companies operate all their power plants (with different sources of energy such as coal, natural gas, hydro, nuclear, and so on) and energy distribution networks to bring the light to our dark room when we turn on the switch.

The same thing is true when we take a glass of water from the kitchen faucet. We do not need to know the details of where the water has come from. We need only to have faith that when we are thirsty we can go to the faucet, turn it on, and fill a glass with clean water. It is indeed very comforting to us, and it takes a great number of worries off our mind, when we know that water and electricity are available when we need them.

When we develop this trust in the Universe, that through its abundance and generosity it has so far taken care of our needs and will continue to do so in the future, many of the negative elements in the happiness equation will be eliminated. For example, if we have perfect trust, the negative elements of anxiety, expectations, fear, greed, guilt, impatience, jealousy, worry and many others will be eliminated. Inversely, the lack of these negative qualities in a person is an indication of his or her faith in the Universe. That is, *one cannot have faith in the operation of the Universe and be worried about things at the same time.*

5. *I do not expect anything from anyone.*

The Universe is my significant *Partner* in providing everything I need. Other people are as much dependent on the Universe for their survival and well-being as I am. When I make use of the best of my knowledge and ability, planning and taking the necessary steps to accomplish something, I have faith in the Universe that it is there, with all its grace and generosity, to accommodate me. I do not expect anything from anyone. I am jealous of no one, and I do not worry and become concerned as to how my needs are to be met; I know that they will. All I need to do is to discover the best service that I can possibly render and then learn how best to plan and carry it out. I have *complete faith* that the Universe will respond, in the most loving and caring ways, to meet my needs. I am always patient for things to happen, as nothing is accomplished instantaneously. It took time for all of us to learn to walk, talk, read, write, and so on. None of these attainments was accomplished instantly. While I may be working and cooperating with other people in a job, I see my job as an opportunity to serve others, and a means by which the Universe meets the needs of myself and my family.

I consider the people I work with, and all other people in my life, to be my teachers in the "University of Life" (3). They are here to teach me the major lessons of this University, which are patience, acceptance, trust and surrender. They therefore provide opportunities for me to live a happier life. These people—be they parents, spouses, or children who may be in my life for as long as 40 to 60 years, or people whom I may meet for only a short time—are in my life as my teachers. They provide opportunities for me to express unconditional love and render unconditional service to them. Thus, they make it possible for me to increase my happiness. In dealing with all of these people in my life, I am always honest and sincere with them, I respect and honor their attitudes and belief systems, and *I accept and love them as they are*.

I consider the material things in my life, although I may have worked hard to acquire them, as gifts from the Universe to meet my needs and to make my life easier. While I am grateful to the Universe for all of these things, I do not become attached to them. I consider them to be mine in trust, and I enjoy having them as long as they are in my life. In case of their departure, I do not feel any grief and sorrow, believing that the Universe will continue to provide for me, in addition to my own efforts, what I need. I make every effort to control my desires, particularly to have no greed and to live modestly. I do so while enjoying all the conveniences that science and technology provide me at this time and place. I am very careful to use as little as possible, to reuse or recycle as much as possible, and to use things that have the least environmental impact.

For those people in my life who have left me, I wish them well, wherever they may go. I send them love, harbor no grudges or resentment toward them, and feel no attachment to them. I believe that they have their own purposes for being here, and that they have had their own lessons to learn in the "University of Life" and therefore must continue to pursue their happiness in their own way.

Let me share with you the following story that I learned when I was in grade school. It deals with the importance of taking the necessary steps or action before the Universe can accommodate our needs.

The lion and the crippled fox. An African man once saw a crippled fox lying under a tree just outside of his village. He wondered how the fox hunted and how he kept alive. He was curious to find out. So he went and hid behind a tree and watched to see what might happen. After a while, he saw a lion, who had hunted a deer, approaching. The man wanted to run away, but decided to stay, believing that the lion had his prey and wouldn't bother him. So he stood there and watched. The lion came very close to where the fox was lying and began eating his dinner. There were no other animals around waiting to scavenge the meat after the lion had his fill. Sure enough, once the lion went on his way, the fox, with some degree of difficulty, crawled to the carcass and had his share of the lion's leftover meal.

The man was astonished to see how a crippled fox was fed. So he thought it would be unnecessary to work any more, believing that, just like the fox, he would be fed too. He stayed home for a couple of days, but nothing happened and nobody gave him any food. He grew very weak and hungry, and he wondered why a fox would be fed and not he. While he was turning this over in his mind, he heard a voice outside his house, which said, "Go and be like a hunting and sharing lion, and not like a crippled fox looking for leftovers and handouts."

6. *It is possible to increase the Universe's generosity, and to learn to receive even more grace from it.*

Is it possible to make the already-generous Universe give more? What are the methods of winning even more favors from this beautiful and abundant Nature of ours? I am sure there are laws for this, too, just as there are laws for many physical phenomena.

For example, there are laws through which we can improve the efficiency of automobiles, light bulbs, and so on. The distance we travel by car today with one gallon or one liter of gasoline is perhaps ten times farther than it was seventy years ago. Humans have learned about new materials and laws through which they can design and build automobiles that use only a small amount of gasoline to go a given distance. The same thing is true about light bulbs, which are much more efficient today. They use significantly less electricity to give the same amount of light as did the bulbs of, say, thirty years ago, and they last longer.

I am sure there are laws that we can employ to increase the generosity of our beloved Nature or Universe, so that it may grant us more of its bounty. Interestingly enough, these laws tie in exactly with all that makes us happier. It is amazing, the more we appreciate, revere, honor, respect, and love Nature and all life forms (including ourselves), the happier we become and the more generous the Universe becomes! Do you remember the vision I shared with you in Chapter 2? It was about a world ruled only by love and respect, happiness and joy, and the Universe was at its peak level of grace. When individually, nationally, and internationally we try to reduce or eliminate hunger and diseases, when all those negative elements of happiness (the misery factors) are eradicated, and when we try to increase our love and gratitude about whatever we have (in the positive elements of happiness), I believe we can expect, and we will be granted, more generosity by our Universe. There is no limit to the possible grace from our already grace-full Universe, which will not only fulfill our material and physical needs, but will grant us unruffled equanimity and bliss. The more we give and the more we care for other beings, or the more UNCONDITIONAL SERVICE we render to others, the more we receive back and the happier we become. In Chapter 7, I will discuss unconditional service as the most significant way of fostering love and reducing or eliminating the negative elements of happiness. But for now, let me share with you the following stories.

A company president gives half of his stock to his employees. About two years ago I gave a seminar in the Phoenix area on the concept of the University of Life. I also talked about the significance of sharing what we have with others. I expressed my own belief that we receive back from the Universe several times more than we invest. A gentleman (Mr. J.G.), while agreeing with what I said, shared his own experience. He said that he was the president of a company that he basically owned. About five years before he had decided simply to give half of his stock in the company to his employees. Everybody thought he was crazy doing so, saying that nobody does things like that. He had assured them that with the rest of his stock he could live very comfortably and that he did not need to worry about anything. He added that, after five years, the value of his stock had risen to ten times what it was before. He explained that, after this action, not only did the employees work better, but an idea came to him, and the company embarked on a brand new venture, which brought a lot of income to it.

A lady gives all the money she has to a needy mother. After the above gentleman shared his experience, I had an opportunity to talk to one of the ladies (Mrs. B.C.) attending the seminar. She said that several years ago, after she had divorced her husband and was taking care of her small children, she had a hard time making ends meet. She worked very hard, driving an old car to work that often broke down and needed repairs. She could not afford to buy a new car or even pay for the repairs of the old one. So what she did was to go to a mechanic who would find out what was wrong with her car and then give her all the tools she needed to work on her own car and fix it. This went on for quite some time, as the car broke down often and needed much attention.

Mrs. B.C. continued that one Sunday afternoon she and her children had gone to a park to enjoy the good weather they were having. Another woman was there with her children, who were playing in the park. Mrs. B.C. heard this woman's children nagging her about being hungry and wanting hamburgers. They complained about eating the same food over and over again at home. She heard this mother telling her children that she did not have any money, and that when they went home, she would fix something different for them to eat. Mrs. B.C. said that she had $20 with her, and that was all the money she had. She decided to give the money to this lady. The woman at first refused to accept the gift. Finally, on Mrs. B.C.'s insistence and her assurance that she didn't need the money then, that her own children were not nagging her to eat out, the other woman finally accepted her gift.

Mrs. B.C. said when she gave the money to this woman, she never thought that the Universe was going to give her back something, or that she was headed for good times in the future, or anything like that. She simply thought that she had the money that could help this woman and she didn't need it for herself.

When she came home with her children that evening and was fixing dinner for them, a young man from the neighborhood supermarket rang her door bell to deliver seven bags of groceries (worth about $150) to her. She at first refused to receive them on the grounds that she had not ordered them. But the young man told her that he had just been given the groceries by one of the store's customers with the address (which was hers) at which to deliver the groceries. He added that he could not take the groceries back, because he did know to whom they belonged.

I asked Mrs. B.C. if she knew where the groceries came from. She said she has not been able to find out for sure, but she thought they may have come from the mechanics at the auto repair shop. They had her home address and perhaps they simply had decided the week before to raise some money for her groceries, and had asked one of their wives to go grocery shopping for that amount.

An honest couple returns a found wallet to its owner. It was late February of 1993 when I read the following story. Later the news made it to local and national television as well.

A woman, Mrs. N., who was walking with her 11-year-old son in a shopping mall in the Los Angeles area, found a wallet. It contained about $2400 in cash, a plane ticket to Hong Kong, a passport, and other documents. She later showed it to her husband and together they decided to turn it in to the police, hoping that the original owner would come to claim it. The owner came and claimed his wallet, thanked this couple and their son, and left for home.

The unique thing about this act and this couple were that both the husband and wife were out of work, had lost their apartment because they could not pay the rent, and slept in their car. They sure could have used the money to meet some of their needs, but chose to do what was right. As I said before, this became a national news item and I followed it in the media. People, upon learning about this couple, their financial difficulties, and their honesty, decided to help. What I learned was that they were both offered jobs, a landlady offered them one of her apartments rent free for six months, and more than $10,000 was sent to them care of the police department by people from all over the U.S. and Canada.

These stories show how the Universe operates. When we give something without expecting anything in return, the Universe, our senior *Partner* in life, returns to us abundantly. We should give, not just the things we no longer need and which we were going to throw out anyway, but the things that we like and can still use. We will not receive the Universe's bounty unless we give of what is dear to us, definitely not like the teenager in the following story:

A mother was lecturing her teenage son to appreciate his food, to finish the food on his plate, and not to waste anything. She added that there are millions of hungry people in the world who would like to have just a portion of what he was eating. The boy, who was half-way through his meal and was no longer hungry, pushed his plate toward his mother, said: "OK, now you can give this to the starving people in Africa."

It is by loving and serving unconditionally and by living righteous lives (lives in which all of the negative elements of happiness are absent) that we can secure more of the Universe's grace in all aspects of our lives and, more important, in *joy and happiness*.

7. *I accept what is happening to me here and now to be the result of my own actions, thoughts, deeds, and wishes that I have put out to the Universe in the past.*

I believe my world is the product of my belief system, and I am what I believe myself to be. My past thoughts, actions, desires, wishes and so on can be considered inputs to the Universe, which, in its great capacity and with extreme grace-fullness, has processed them and provided what is happening to me here and now. I should not feel guilty for the "mistakes" that I have made, realizing that they were necessary for my learning process in the "University of Life." After all, a first year medical student who cannot perform surgery as his professor does, has not committed any sins. He simply doesn't know how yet. Given sufficient time, based on his efforts, he will learn to perform surgeries. He may even become a better surgeon than his professor.

This belief, that what happens to us is the result of our own actions, is quite different from the concept of fatalism. Let me share with you the following examples to illustrate the meaning of the above statement.

A student taking an exam in a thermodynamics course. I have taught thermodynamics for many years now. This is a required course in mechanical engineering education in all universities. Depending on the number of students, the course may be offered in several sections during every semester or quarter.

A student graduating from high school decides whether or not he wants to go to college. He or she may even have decided already to study mechanical engineering or another profession. The student applies to several universities which have this field of study. If his or her grade point average is high enough, the student may be accepted to a number of universities. The student happens to choose to attend the one where I teach. He or she takes and passes all the prerequisite courses and is finally ready to sign up for the course of thermodynamics. Out of many sections of the course offered, this student decides to register for the one I am teaching that semester.

It has been my practice to announce, on the first day of each class that I teach, how I intend to teach the course, what materials will be covered and in how many lecture hours, when the examinations will be, and so on. I will also tell the students what materials will be covered in each exam, how I intend to grade the students' performances, and that I expect them not to come to class late. I announce these plans ahead of time so that if they don't like my method of handling the course, they can drop it and sign up for another section before it is too late.

On the announced day of examination, the student comes to the room and is handed the questions to answer. He or she may not enjoy taking an exam that hour or that day, or answering a particular question, but there are no other choices. Without taking the examination as scheduled and answering the questions asked, certain consequences will have to be faced. Now, is the student forced to take the exam and answer the questions asked? I do not think so. Note that the student has exercised many choices such as going to college, studying mechanical engineering, coming to this university, taking the section of the course of thermodynamics that I am teaching, staying in my section after learning how I planned to conduct the course, and each step leading up to the exam. After making all these choices, the university system provided all the rest, including arranging for the exam to be held on that hour and on that day. The student was not forced to do anything.

The same thing is true in the "University of Life" (3); we make choices and the Universe provides. So everything that is happening to me now is the result of my own choices (including my desires, thoughts, actions, wishes, etc.) that I have made before. I may not remember them, but the Universe with its infinite memory does. I am fully responsible for all that is happening to me now.

A "billion-line" computer program to describe the order and behavior of the Universe. Let me borrow from the language of computer programming to illustrate the above point. If we knew all the laws of the Universe, and if we could describe them in mathematical form, we could perhaps write a computer program to describe the behavior of the Universe. To me, this would be at least a one-billion line program. It would have to account for everything—physics, chemistry, biology, sociology, economics, spirituality, people's behavior, particularly their faith and belief systems about the Universe, and so on. Our thoughts and actions are like sitting in front of a computer terminal that is connected to this huge computer, which displays many options from which to choose. As soon as I make a choice, the program runs and, after some time, depending on the nature of my chosen option, it gives me an answer. To me, this imaginary billion-line computer program reflects the order of the Universe. I constantly make choices which are inputted to this "people-friendly" computer program, and after a while it gives me the results of my choices. In other words, "I reap what I have sown." Or, *I am the product of my past actions and the architect of my future*. It is indeed like the profession of architecture. At first an architect has a thought. He takes the necessary steps, with the Universe contributing in a big way (supplying all the materials and products that he needs) to accommodate him and bring about what he had envisaged before.

By my actions, thoughts, desires, and wishes for myself and others, I am designing my future, and inviting into my life all that is going to happen to me later on. It is therefore extremely important that I do not resort to violence or wish ill toward anyone and do nothing that will harm anybody or anything, physically or emotionally. Instead, I respect, honor, revere, and love all beings, including myself. I know that by these choices I will be "putting in an order" for a pleasant and joyous life for myself in the immediate and distant futures.

8. *I accept what happens to me here and now as having been provided by the Universe and that it is the best possible outcome for my long-range interest and well-being.*

The beautiful thing about this Universe, or this "computer program," is that it is very "friendly." I do not understand all the laws of the Universe or all the lines of this huge "computer program," but I can trust that it has my well-being in mind, along with the well-being of all other beings. It is impossible for a loving, generous, and gracious Universe to provide something bad. It is only because of my limited knowledge that I might call things bad or inappropriate. I need to consider my long-range interests, and not just my immediate "gain." The Universe is designed to maximize my happiness, taking into account all the choices I have made.

9. *I am always content, not critical, with the results of my actions.*

When I want something, but it does not come about, I accept what has happened, believing that this will be better for me. Or, I accept the outcomes as a lesson of the "University of Life," realizing that perhaps I need to plan differently to reach my goal. If people who have been involved with me seem not to have played their roles fairly, and it seems that they are responsible for my failure, under no circumstances do I become distraught, upset, or angry at anyone or about anything. I do not hate anyone, nor do I make any judgment about anyone's character. I do not gossip about or wish ill for anyone, or plan vengeance against anyone, or resort to violence. I use my best judgment to plan again to achieve what I want, and under all circumstances I consider other people's and other beings' welfare when I make decisions that affect them.

When I accomplish something, and when my needs are met, I realize that this has been the result of my actions and the Universe's cooperation, just like the farmer and the Universe cooperate for an apple seed to become a tree and produce a certain variety of apple. While I feel good for having accomplished something, under no circumstances do I become arrogant or deserving of all the credit. I continually express my gratitude—internally in my heart to the Universe, for its generosity and grace, and externally to all those who have helped and cooperated to make this accomplishment possible.

10. *The well-being of the environment, the entire planet Earth, and all beings (particularly humans), affects my emotional state and happiness.*

In increasing or maximizing my happiness, I cannot be complacent about other people's happiness or miseries, and other being's welfare. That is, not only do I accept the right of other beings to live on this planet as I do, but I respect and revere all life forms. I do not harm anybody or anything, and I do whatever

I can to make sure that they too have happy lives. I do this out of respect for all other beings, realizing that their well-being affects my own happiness and joy in life.

It is a fact that all beings on planet Earth originated from the same source. Physically, we are all made of the same materials that came into being at the time of the Big Bang, or when the Universe started. For nearly 15 billion years all kinds of changes have taken place in the Universe to bring about all that is found on Earth today. All these materials are recycled over and over again. For example, a molecule of water in my body may have already been in millions of other life forms on the planet. The same is true about the other elements constituting my body.

The oneness of all beings is not limited to their physical bodies alone. All beings and all life forms are manifestations of only one Being, which existed before the Big Bang and now prevails as well. It prevails not only in all beings' physical dimensions, but also in their emotional, mental, and spiritual bodies. In other words, all the five billion people, billions and billions of other life forms, and all of the "non-living" entities are faces or manifestations of the same thing. Viewed in this way, we are clearly all members of the same "body," and not separate from each other. It is only right, therefore, that I care about the other "elements" of my body, and not just for other human beings, animals, and plants, but also the entire environment.

I believe it is a law of the Universe that the well-being and happiness of all beings are interconnected to one another. It is hard to prove this scientifically, but I believe the well-being of people, animals, plants, and other beings everywhere affects my own well-being and happiness. We all have noticed how the suffering or joy of people around us affects us. However, we do not have to "witness" such an emotional state in a person to be affected by it; the suffering or joy of all people and all beings everywhere in the world affects our emotional state, and will reduce or increase our happiness. So, for our own well-being and happiness, we need to help eradicate all forms of human suffering, including hunger, malnutrition, disease, oppression, ignorance, the suffering of animals due to the loss of their habitats or environmental pollution, and the suffering of plant life caused by the degradation of the ecosystem.

Going back to the question of attitude and belief system raised at the beginning of this chapter, I shared with you a few stories illustrating how having faith in a doctor or medicine can overcome sickness and disease. It is now generally accepted that without the faith of the patient in a certain diagnosis, he or she cannot be cured through such a treatment. Now, what role does faith play in other matters, especially how the ten attitudes or beliefs discussed in this chapter may play out in our lives? I mentioned that developing these ten beliefs is the most important and difficult task in acquiring happiness. Let me share with you how my own attitudes and beliefs helped me to be a successful salesman during my student years.

My successful career as an encyclopedia salesman. During the summer of 1960, I worked as an encyclopedia salesman in St. Louis, Missouri. I was a graduate student at the University of Illinois, and had decided to come to St. Louis, instead of going to Chicago, to look for a summer job. I tried hard to get a job with an engineering company so that I could learn something in the line of my studies, but there weren't too many companies hiring students for the summer. An ad in a local paper lured me into joining a firm and becoming an outstanding encyclopedia salesman, not only in the St. Louis area, but also throughout the entire Midwest. When I look back now, I attribute my success to my faith and belief system about what I was doing. The company had taught us (me and all the students working for them over summer) that we were not selling *any* encyclopedia, but by "placing" a few sets in selected homes, we were promoting and advertising the set. The company made us believe that we were doing a big favor to these people. This was the company's sales pitch. It was a presentation that the company had spent a lot of time developing, and we all had to memorize it and know it by heart.

Being very naive and optimistic, I believed this pitch. When I went to people's homes to make a presentation, not only did I repeat all the lines that I had memorized, but, more important, I did it with a great deal of sincerity and enthusiasm. I really had the belief that I was doing a great favor to people to "place" a complete set of this beautiful encyclopedia in their home. Even though I had to go door-to-door to meet the prospective receivers, I was always treated courteously by people. Maybe my love of meeting and talking to people, together with my belief that I was doing them a great favor, helped me to receive such treatment. Other student-salesmen were not as lucky as I was. Many were kicked out of homes after the people learned what they were doing, or simply were not allowed to enter their homes to talk to them. But none of those things happened to me. In fact, many people invited me to have dinner with them later.

For the first ten weeks of summer everything went very well, and I "placed" many sets of encyclopedias and made a lot of money. In fact, I made twice as much money as I did the summer before while working as a mechanical engineer in Milwaukee, Wisconsin. I made enough money to buy my first car. Then, for the last two weeks of summer (before going back to the university), I did not sell anything at all. What happened was that I learned from the company's vice-president (who was visiting our office and giving a pep talk to promote the sales) that we were just selling the encyclopedia, and not favoring anybody at all by "placing" a set at their homes. I learned that what the people paid was actually the regular price of the set and not, as we were taught to believe and tell the people we visited, less than one-third of its bookstore price. This shattered my "faith" and belief system to the point that I was unable to make any more sales for the rest of the summer. I still went door-to-door every night, making the same presentation as before, but it was not the same. Now my new attitude and belief system made people intuitively realize that what I was telling them was just another sales pitch, and they were not interested.

Before, there must have been something more than just the words I was saying that made people buy a set of encyclopedias from me. I am sure that my positive attitude, enthusiasm, and my "faith" and belief were responsible for my success. Now that those had vanished, my success also ended.

So how does a belief system work? For the patient who has faith in his doctor, maybe it is the operation of the brain and other organs that produce the needed chemicals to heal a certain illness. But how was it in my case? Could it be that through my positive attitude and "faith" I was communicating with the Universe better, and the Universe made all the arrangements by affecting the opinions and thoughts of all those people I was communicating with, to like me and be willing to buy a set of encyclopedias from me?

We saw in the examples of farming and flying at the beginning of this chapter that the Universe is a big or senior Partner with us in our endeavors. I believe our "faith" is the means by which we communicate with our big Partner. It is our link and "telephone" communication with the Universe, acknowledging its great and generous contribution to our partnership. When we raise our share of stock slightly in the partnership (for example, by serving someone unconditionally), our big Partner makes a grand contribution toward the joint venture. For every simple act of service that I render, which may be nothing more than bringing a little joy into someone's life, my big Partner increases its share of the process by one million times, giving me more joy and happiness.

Summary of Developing a Proper Attitude and Belief System

I believe that by developing "faith" in the ten attitudes presented in this chapter, we can eliminate all the negative elements of happiness (the elements of misery) listed in Chapter 3. It is an important way to maintain a constant communication with the Universe, affirming our commitment and willingness to stay in the partnership. It is a joint venture wherein, by our giving a little, our big Partner, the Universe, gives its share of a million to one, and grants us JOY and HAPPINESS.

6

LOVE: THE KEY ELEMENT
IN ACHIEVING HAPPINESS

*Start the day with love, fill the day with love, and end the day
with love. Love is the Supreme Mark of Humanness.*

—Sri Sathya Sai Baba

Life without love is void and empty.

Without a doubt, love has been the most talked about subject
in human history. Love is the thing that makes the world go
around. Love is life and life is love. Love is that unselfish, loyal,
and benevolent concern that you have for the well-being of your
beloved. Love is that state or emotion in which whatever you see,
think, feel, or want is your beloved. You are so deeply absorbed in
your beloved that there is no more you—only him, her, or it. You
are willing to give everything you have, including your life, for
your beloved, and you want nothing in return for yourself.

Love is often used in conjunction with sex. "Making love" or
having sex is the satisfaction of a physical need, whereas loving
someone or something is the satisfaction of an emotional need. It
is ideal for married couples when these two are combined.

It is because of the importance of love in one's happiness that,
in the Happinometry equation, I arbitrarily selected 70 points (out
of a total of 100 for all the positive elements of happiness) for love.

To many people who have been deeply in love, and who have felt the bliss and tranquillity that are associated with deep love, even this value is low. By arbitrarily selecting a value like this, I wanted to give some credit to the other factors that can bring us joy in life (see the list on page 27). For those who may think that 70 points are too many, I would like to emphasize that without love, the happiness and joy of life are minimal. Particularly, in its absence, the negative elements may become dominant and wipe out all one's positive points from accomplishment, contentment, forgiveness, gratitude, hope, optimism, recognition, and well-wishfullness.

When a deep, or "70-point," love prevails in our lives, practically all of the negative elements discussed in Chapter 3 are eliminated. I know that, with a 70-point love present in my life, the miseries of anger, arrogance, attachment, fear, greed, gossip, jealousy, resentment, vengeance, violence, worry, and all other negative emotions will all be eliminated. With such a deep state of love, nothing can disturb me, because I will see my "beloved" in everyone and everything.

History records the decisions of kings and wealthy people who gave up their social positions and material possessions for love. Books have been written about the power of love and the miracles it performs in one's life. During a talk show, while trying to explain his philosophy of healing to a group of doctors, Dr. Bernie Siegel (4) said, "You see, I love them, and then they start to get well." Mother Theresa, after her success in "taking care of the poorest of the poor" in India, decided to expand her activities to New York City. When told that there aren't that many destitutes in New York City, she replied, "That is true, there aren't too many people hungry for food, but there are many who are hungry for love."

How do we develop love? One thing is certain; we cannot buy it with money or acquire it through fame and political or social power. Love is a quality in every one of us—*we are born with love*. We, as a part of a loving Universe, already possess love. It is something we do not need to acquire from someone or somewhere else. All we need to do is foster it and allow it to flow. We need to eliminate all that hides love and prevents it from "glowing" and showing.

I believe that by adopting the belief system described in the previous chapter and by reducing, and eventually eliminating, the negative elements of happiness, more and more love will appear.

Love may be likened to a giant light bulb connected to a huge power plant through an intricate network called "faith." The only reason my light bulb doesn't shine is that it is covered by all kinds of "dirt," such as arrogance, attachment, cynicism, resentment or grudges, guilt, hate, hypocrisy, jealousy, violence, worry, and so on (all the elements of misery). Once I succeed in cleansing myself of this "dirt," then love will start shining and radiating to others. The question is, how can I cleanse myself of all this "dirt," or get rid of all those elements of misery? Before trying to find an answer to this very important question, let me first share with you the following vision I had in India.

The Bird that Flies on Wings of Love and Service

In January of 1990 I was in India for a visit with Sri Sathya Sai Baba, followed by giving a few seminars at two universities in India, one in Bangalore and one in Indore. This was my sixth visit to India, but the second with this Master. My first visit with Sai Baba took place about 16 months earlier and was very short. This time, I was planning to stay longer, and I anticipated and hoped for a personal interview during which I could ask a question. Essentially I wanted to ask how I could best increase my joy and happiness in life. I had read many self-help books and had attended numerous seminars with the focus on how to be more in touch with one's feelings. Although I had been helped by such books and seminars, it appeared that I needed to take more seminars and read more books. There were so many more books to read and seminars to take that I thought I could never catch up with all of them, let alone find the time and money needed to invest in them. I thought there must be a short cut to my quest for happiness.

So, here was my chance to ask Sai Baba the question that had been bothering me for some time. I felt that I needed to meet Him in person and ask my question, never thinking that other means of communication were also possible. It was through one of these "other" means that Sai Baba addressed my inquiry on the very first night I spent in His compound.

I was trying to rest from a long and tiring journey and sleep on a very thin mattress placed in the middle of a large dormitory hall. It was difficult, because almost all the other seventy-nine foreign men in the hall were snoring (everyone in his own language)! Furthermore, I couldn't sleep because I was very excited about my visit with Sai Baba, and the opportunity that I was hoping to have to talk to and ask Him my question. While I was lying down, still hearing and quite disturbed by all the background noises, I "saw" in my mind the picture of a bird, flying upward from right to left. It was like a slide projection on a large screen. On the left wing of this bird was written LOVE and on the right, SERVICE. Here was my answer. In our quest for happiness, we are like birds, needing two wings with which to fly. Just like birds, who cannot fly with just one wing, we too need to have the two wings—one of LOVE and one of SERVICE—to fly directly to joy, happiness, and bliss. Then I saw that to the feet of the bird were attached a number of weights: anger, arrogance, desire, fear, gossip, greed, hate, hypocrisy, jealousy, lust, pride, vengeance, violence, worry and so on. Now, here was the total, and the most complete, answer to my question.

To move upwards, to fly, to have ultimate joy and happiness in life, I need to strengthen my wings of LOVE and SERVICE and make every effort to drop all those weights, or at least to reduce their sizes. I was watching this picture, while I was completely aware of all the background noises in the hall. Then I realized that these three elements, that is, Love, Service and the dropping of the weights, are interrelated, in that, by strengthening my love and service, I could easily reduce or drop all those weights. Someone with unconditional love, translated into unconditional service, is not jealous of anyone, does not gossip about anyone, and doesn't hate anyone. It is with deep love that one can drop all these weights and be liberated. On the other hand, with the lack of hate, hypocrisy, jealousy, gossip and so on, one's love toward others automatically increases. Then another question came to me: which one of these elements do I need to work on first? Which one must I start accomplishing first, Love or the dropping of the weights? Or, is there a way that I can accomplish both? I felt there must be an answer. However, nothing more came during this vision and experience.

I must have spent a few hours after the vision, or the "slide presentation," before I finally fell asleep, assimilating the knowledge that, I believe, summarizes the teaching of all the Masters who have ever taught humanity how to live. The next morning, I still wondered about my new question. A couple of days after this vision, I was among a group called in for an interview with Sai Baba, but there was no chance for me to ask that question. It was a couple of weeks later that I finally received my answer, again indirectly. In a very interesting and blissful way, the final answer came to the question of how best to foster love and at the same time drop all those weights of misery: the answer is SERVICE.

Yes, UNCONDITIONAL, SELFLESS, and
LOVING SERVICE.

7

UNCONDITIONAL SERVICE: THE SUREST WAY TO INCREASE LOVE AND REDUCE MISERY

Selfless service is the fragrant flower of altruistic love.
It is not to be performed for the satisfaction of the person
rendering the service. Man should regard selfless service
as the purpose for which he is given life.

—Sri Sathya Sai Baba

Here is the opportunity to both foster love and get rid of all those elements of misery:

JUST SERVE UNCONDITIONALLY.

We can find many people who, without seeking any publicity or fanfare, spend their time helping others. We may wonder whether they enjoy their work, or if they are happy. I would like to share with you the following experience concerning a young medical doctor who dedicated his time and income to serve the needy. This doctor was very happy and felt honored for the opportunity.

A psychiatrist who felt honored to serve. About 25 years ago I met a young psychiatrist who was very much involved in the service of needy people. Dr. E.S. had been out of medical school for a few years when he visited a mental institution. He was appalled by the condition of the mental patients and with the treatment they were receiving. He decided to do something about it. He encouraged his wealthy father to build a small institution in which he could render dignified and proper treatment to the patients who were suffering from, as he called it, the worst illness in the world. After his father's death, using funds from his inheritance, he expanded the hospital and admitted more patients. He also expanded his activities and initiated a charitable organization, based on an elaborate program of identifying and helping to meet the needs of poor people in his town. He emphasized serving the children of these people, so the children could receive both proper nutrition and education.

Dr. E.S. was against handouts to those who could work. Therefore, he determined to start up small manufacturing and production facilities to create jobs for people whose self-esteem and dignity had been shattered due to joblessness. To the poor people who could not work, he provided food, clothing, and school supplies for their children. He was against giving them money, for fear the money would be used for unnecessary things. Another advantage of not giving people money lay in the fact that he could buy needed materials in large quantities and receive a large discount from manufacturers and suppliers. He knew many suppliers and manufacturers; through his artful persuasion and because of the charitable nature of his activities, he used to receive large discounts from them. He was well known in the community; however, he did not care about gaining fame and preferred to serve anonymously.

When I met Dr. E.S., he was in the process of purchasing a large parcel of land outside the town to expand his activities in small-scale manufacturing and agricultural jobs, for those who could work but could not get a job elsewhere. This, he explained, would provide the needed income for his projects, as well as assistance to the needy. He also considered these activities to be therapy for his patients. He used to call his new place "the psychiatric village."

I have followed Dr. E.S.'s activities all these years. He began an elaborate agricultural and industrial program in the "village," growing wheat and other grains, raising cattle and sheep, and erecting buildings to house his small-scale industries. I used to spend about one afternoon a week with Dr. E.S. as a consultant on his industrial projects, listening to his new programs and, frankly, becoming charged with enthusiasm and joy. Every time I met him, he had a new program going. He used to say, "If you have a project of good cause to carry out, do not worry about the money; never worry where it is going to come from. The Universe, with its infinite generosity, will provide." His accomplishments were testimonies to this statement.

He kept on admitting more mental patients (usually poor patients who would not be accepted by other hospitals), added a retarded children's division to care for children who could not be taken care of by their parents, and so on. He utilized the labor of his patients as much as possible while paying them fair wages for their work.

It became a weekly event for me to drive a relatively long distance to go to see Dr. E.S. in the "village." I talked about his activities in my classes and shared his enthusiasm and joy with my students. Often, students came along with me to meet Dr. E.S. and learn how he carried out his welfare projects. Many of these students then became involved with assisting him on his projects. A few of the women students provided love and nurturing to the retarded children.

Dr. E.S. worked about 80 hours per week, with no holiday or vacation. He was often criticized by his colleagues that he was crazy to work so much—not to make enough money, not to live as "comfortably" as they did, and not to save anything for his future. Dr. E.S. would reply by asking them how they spent their time and the money they made. They would answer that they work about 40 hours a week, have comfortable lifestyles, save enough money to travel to Europe and other places about one month of the year to have a good time, and enjoy themselves.

Dr. E.S. would reply, "You are happy only one month of the year; I am happy all twelve months of the year. I enjoy immensely what I am doing; *it is a great honor and privilege for me to serve* these poor and dejected people." Dr. E.S. and his family lived very modestly, not at all like other doctors in town. However, I knew that he and his family really enjoyed what they were doing, and they were very happy to help the poor people of the town, as well as many mental patients and retarded children who were sent to them from all over the country. I consider meeting Dr. E.S. a major event in my life. One of Dr. E.S.'s blessings was to have a wife and family who were as interested in helping others as he was.

It is indeed a great fortune and honor to be able to serve others. To maximize our happiness, we should look for every opportunity to serve. We should not seek recognition and praise from anyone or any source; we shouldn't even think of the joy that such service will bring. Just to give selflessly, to do so as a duty and be proud and honored by it, will bestow immense joy. As Mother Theresa put it, "Nothing makes you feel happier than when you really reach out in mercy to someone who is badly hurt."

We should search for opportunities to serve and seek anonymity for our actions. We need always to be vigilant in finding the right time for our actions, and do so anonymously, seeking no recognition.

With the development of the proper attitude and belief system, and with the fostering of unconditional love, which translates only into unconditional service, there is nothing in the world that can prevent us from attaining the highest possible level of happiness and joy. Returning to the example of a bird that flies on wings of LOVE and SERVICE, with all those "weights" or miseries dropped, and with the wings of LOVE and SERVICE strengthened, we can soar high in joy, happiness and bliss—a height for which there is no limit.

Choice of Career and Profession

By the work we do for a living, we know whether we are rendering any service or not. However, is this the best we can and should do? Each one must answer this question for him or herself. We all change jobs and look for better opportunities. When we change one job for another, are we looking for higher pay, more fulfilling work (where we feel a greater sense of accomplishment), or for an opportunity to serve more effectively? It is ideal to have all three motivations. Then, in case we need to make choices, are we willing to adopt a modest lifestyle and give up some conveniences in order to be more useful?

Wouldn't it be wonderful if the only criterion for us to choose a career was rendering unconditional service most effectively? It would be great if this were also the only reason for us to study and go on into higher education. We need not worry about having enough food to eat, or having a nice home in which to live, or having more conveniences of life to enjoy. We need only be concerned as to how we can most effectively render unconditional service. The Universe with its abundance and grace provides for us and will sustain us.

I believe a young person or a student planning a career should consider his or her interests, talents, and abilities to see how he or she can best serve and be useful to society. One should prepare for this career as best as one can, always having in mind the service to be rendered upon completion of one's studies.

As an additional means of fostering love and service, we should recognize and acknowledge the work of the great servants of society, both in history and in current times. Their lifestyles and contributions in bringing joy and comfort to humanity and other beings on the planet should be documented and brought to the attention of the world, and these people should be celebrated formally as heroes and heroines. As a means of such recognition, perhaps the first weekend of each month could be dedicated to such recognition, with each of the following weekends allocated to a specific type of service.

Exercise 10. *List the world servers whom you like to have recognized and honored as heroes or heroines in Love and Service.*

Rendering service is nothing but the bringing of joy and happiness into someone's life. Our first priority must be to care for the people who are in our immediate surroundings and have the most in common with us. However, we should always be careful that under the slogan of "helping our families" or "serving our country," our actions and services do not have any adverse effect on other people or beings of the world, and under no circumstance ought our actions to hurt them. After all, every being in the world has as much right to be happy as I, my family, and my countrymen do.

I hope to reach that level of love and spiritual awareness to consider all humankind my brothers and sisters, and all other forms of life my "cousins."

8

THE VITAL PRACTICE
OF LINKING WITH A MASTER

You can live without something, if you have someone to live for.
—Robert H. Schuller

In Exercise 8 of Chapter 5, I asked you to identify one or more people whom you thought were very loving, serving, and happy. Now, think again about these people, and see who are the ones you believe have done the most effective service.

Many scientists and engineers, through various discoveries or inventions, have truly helped mankind, and many such inventions were made in this century, so I am sure you can think of at least a few names. These people's work opened up new areas of science and technology for us to explore and become appreciative of the splendor and magnificence of the Universe, but their most significant contributions have been to make life easier and more comfortable. When we spend less time taking care of our physical needs, we presumably have more time to spend on the more subtle aspects of life, namely on emotional and spiritual growth. We are grateful to these people and the Universe for all of these advances and contributions.

Exercise 11: *Think of all the discoveries and inventions throughout history that you believe have had the most significant impact on our lifestyle, such as fire, electricity, the automobile, and others. Write down at least 20 such things, and see if you can identify a person with each of them. Organize your list in order of importance. This would be an interesting high-school project, where the findings of all the students can be compared and shared at the end.*

I certainly respect and honor the work of discoverers, inventors, scientists, and engineers, and I admire the work of those who teach us how to make a living (as all teachers in the educational systems do). However, I believe the work of those people throughout history who have taught us how to live and how to be happy, is much more significant. I would like to refer to these people as Master Teachers, or just Masters.

I believe it is a law of the Universe that, once we think of someone or something for a long time, we acquire some of their qualities and characteristics. These Masters, because of their immense and unconditional love, their selfless service, and their lack of all those elements of misery (see Chapter 3), are, in my opinion, the happiest people who ever lived. Applying the Happinometry equation to them, they all get a perfect score of 100. I can name Moses, Jesus, Mary, Mohammed, Zoroaster, Rama, Krishna, Buddha, Gandhi, Yogananda, and others who have lived before, and among the living Masters, Sai Baba, Mother Theresa, and so on. In the context of the University of Life (3), these Masters can be called the Visiting Professors.

In our pursuit of happiness, I believe it is most advantageous to think of these Masters often, and to mentally link with at least one of them on a regular basis.

I am sure you know how the mind travels from one subject to another. You may be different, but my mind is always on the run; it is like a monkey, always jumping from one branch to another. My mind is always occupied, but not very often with the things with which I prefer it to be. We use our mind for a relatively small portion of time to think about the work we do. The rest of the time it is a "monkey mind." If I can train my mind, during its "spare" time, to be directed toward one of these Masters, I know I will gain many benefits in my pursuit of happiness.

By constantly keeping the thought of a Master in mind, I know that I can attain some of the Master's qualities, particularly the immense love and the desire to serve unconditionally. This will also help me to reduce and gradually eliminate all of the elements of misery. That is, along with my rendering unconditional service and along with my other efforts to reduce those negative elements of happiness, I can use the linkage with a Master as a supplement to help me gradually drop all those weights of misery that hinder my flight to a happier life. Such a linkage helps me redirect my mind from running around all over the place, and instead focus on someone who is a symbol of love and service—someone whose life has been total bliss. I can then increase my joy and happiness.

Exercise 12: *Name at least three Masters for whom you have great respect and admiration. List their names here, and underline the one you are most specifically fond of and can most easily relate to:*

I should emphasize the supplementary nature of such a linkage for joyous living. It cannot substitute for selfless service. In another words, I cannot sit at home and try to make contact with these Masters, hoping for happiness. All these Masters kept busy serving others with love and compassion. I cannot, therefore, bypass service. I can only employ such a linkage as a supplement to service, and not as a substitute for it.

Another benefit of such a linkage is the ability to ask these Master Educators the questions that we cannot find answers to, or to ask them to help us solve problems with which we are faced. I have had a number of experiences where "linkage" with a Master helped me to solve problems.

Linkage with a Master to solve a problem. About three years ago, a student came to my office to see his final examination papers. Although he had passed the course, he was not happy with it. In fact he was very sad and extremely upset when he came in. He spent about ten minutes going through all the questions and then handed the papers back to me. I asked him if he had any questions or any objections to the way I had graded him. He said he did not have any objections to my grading, but he was very upset about making stupid mistakes in all of his exams. As a result, all of his grades were barely passing. He added that he had studied hard during the semester for all of his exams and knew the material, but he did not receive the grades he deserved.

I did not have an answer to his predicament. So, I decided to link with a Master and to mentally ask Him to provide an answer to this student's problem. This was similar to someone coming to me for an answer to a question for which I do not have the answer, in which case I decide to call up someone more knowledgeable than myself. I did the same thing here. I linked with the Master mentally, asking Him to please answer this young man's question. While waiting for my "long distance call" to go through, I looked at and listened to the young man, who was elaborating on his predicament, as though he was my son and the dearest person in my life. I simply exuded love toward him. It took about ten minutes before something came to my mind as the answer to his problem. I was pleased with it and shared it with the student, who was almost finished with the disclosure of his difficulties. The answer was basically that he should not think so much about his failures and about making so many mistakes during his examinations. Instead, he should go into his exams with a very positive attitude and the belief that he is going to do very well on them. He should also visualize coming out of the examination room, completely satis-fied with his performance, and later on receiving his examination papers back with very good marks. I then elaborated that he ought to find a quiet time and place every morning to sit down, close his eyes, take several deep breaths, and repeat the above affirmations and visualizations. The student liked the idea and left my office happier and smiling—not at all like his appearance when he had come in about twenty minutes earlier.

I have had other similar experiences, when I did not know exactly what to do. I had employed all avenues and means of solving a particular problem, without getting anywhere. Then, I decided to ask a Master. After waiting and being patient, and at the same time sending love to all concerned, an answer came. This was similar to a student spending a lot of time thinking about a problem, but not being able to solve it. Finally, he or she goes to his or her "professor" for help. The important thing in such a linkage is thinking or visualizing the Master you love and to whom you easily relate, and mentally posing the question to Him or Her. In the meantime, you simply wait and send love to all the people or the situation concerned. Try to be calm and focus your mind on the Master. This linkage is most effective if you can be completely relaxed. For this purpose you can sit down in a quiet place, close your eyes, take several deep breaths, and visualize the Master as being with you. Then, mentally pose the question you have to Him or Her. Express thanks for the opportunity to ask the question and then wait patiently for an answer—it may take ten or twenty minutes or so. In any case, if an answer comes, accept it with gratitude. If nothing comes, still be content that you had an opportunity to calm and relax yourself. Then be vigilant as you go about your activities, for a sign or thought may come to you which you will recognize as an answer to your question. You may not get an answer immediately, but your sincere questions will be answered.

I once read an incident concerning a devotee of Sri Sathya Sai Baba. This lady, along with many others, was in grave danger of losing her life during the hijacking of an airplane. When she "linked" with Sai Baba, she heard Him telling her to send love to all those who were threatening her. Because of her immense love and trust for Sai Baba, she was able to do as He had instructed her. She became calm and looked at the men who were threatening her life as if they were her own children. She radiated love toward them. After a while, the hijackers decided to surrender; the danger passed, and she and the others with her were saved.

I believe loving a Master and being able to relate and link to Him or Her, should not be limited just to times when we have hard problems which we cannot solve. We should always try to keep the thoughts of a Master in mind and connect with Him or Her. Such a linkage will give us calmness and serenity, and will bring love and respect, acceptance and understanding of all beings. It also helps us to gradually reduce the elements of misery and to increase the positive elements of happiness.

Linkage with a Master as the Nourishment for the "Love-and-Service" Bird

You may recall the vision I shared with you in Chapter 6. This happened when I was visiting with Sri Sathya Sai Baba in India in January of 1990. It involved the picture of the LOVE and SERVICE bird, showing that in our quest for happiness we are like a bird, needing to use both our wings of LOVE and SERVICE "to fly"—to acquire happiness.

About a month after I had left India, I received more revelations from this Master. I learned that the connection or linkage with a Master, or keeping the thought of a Master in mind, is like the food and nourishment that we, as birds searching for happiness and joy, need to have in order to be able to fly to attain what we are here to accomplish.

I am now making an effort to maintain a connection with a Master often, or at least any time that I am in a difficult situation or need to make a difficult decision. I like to call this exercise "having a meeting with my Friend and Master." I ask Him for His guidance.

Exercise 13: *Consider the Master you identified earlier. He or She is the one who symbolizes immense love and unconditional service to you. Now try to relate, link, and communicate with this Master as if He or She were present with you at all times and in all places. You can contact and talk to the Master at any time and in any place. These Masters are never too busy to respond. They are like those professors who are always available to help their students solve their problems. So, talk to your Master. If you are alone, you may even want to talk to Him or Her aloud. Otherwise, in order that other people not think that you are weird talking to yourself, link with your Master mentally. Because you may get side-tracked during normal hours, at first you may want to set aside a quiet period for such a "conversation." The more relaxed you are, and the more centered you are, the better will be your connection and linkage with the Master. When you have relaxed yourself, try imagining that this Master is with you in a beautiful garden, sharing a bench, or walking along a lovely path, ready to converse with you and answer your questions.*

I suggest that you make this communication at least once a day, preferably early in the morning. Sit in a quiet place, close your eyes, take a few deep breaths, and visualize your Master as being with you. Review all the tasks you need to perform during the day, and ask Him or Her to tell you the best ways to perform them. Wait for His or Her answer.

9

TEN GUARANTEED WAYS TO FURTHER INCREASE HAPPINESS

It is neither wealth nor splendor, but tranquility and occupations,
which give happiness.

—Thomas Jefferson

When work is pleasure, life is a joy.

—Maxim Gorky

In the previous four chapters we discussed the most effective means of acquiring happiness and joy in life, the most important being the fostering of unconditional love through the rendering of unconditional service. Besides Love, with its unparalleled impact on happiness, the Happinometry equation contains other positive elements—accomplishment, contentment, forgiveness, gratitude, hope, optimism, recognition and well-wishfulness. Each of these elements of happiness is potent in its own right toward alleviating personal miseries and increasing one's joy.

Accomplishment and Recognition

We always enjoy accomplishing something, feeling good that something has resulted from all the time and energy spent. Without this sense of accomplishment, life becomes dull.

The joy of accomplishment may result from discovering new phenomena or laws of nature, solving a problem or puzzle, or inventing a machine or device. It happens when a mother makes dinner for her family, helps her children with their homework, makes something for her family, and so on. It includes the feeling one gets from designing and building something, making a tangible contribution, creating something, or fulfilling any goal. Joy of accomplishment may also be fostered by bringing about a change in lifestyle, for example, buying something needed such as a car or a house, or improving one's lifestyle by adding more conveniences, and so on. Winning an intellectual or sports competition or physical gratification may also be classified under the broad category of accomplishment. For many, simply working diligently to make a living and providing for their families gives them the joy of accomplishment.

All people need to work, not just to make a living, but to have a sense of accomplishment and self-worth, to know that their work matters. We ought to look for jobs that are not only useful to society, but that also give us this sense of contribution or accomplishment. Many successful business executives have learned that by creating a work environment where employees have more control in defining their own goals and working hours, and the opportunity to participate in the company's decision-making process, the business prospers. Managers of such companies have found that, through such freedom and participation, and with proper recognition, employees feel a greater sense of personal worth, have greater job satisfaction and, as a result, have more loyalty and increase their productivity. Employees who feel their work matters are happier and have fewer absences from the work place because they are also healthier.

Several years ago I read in the papers that Swiss youth in large cities were holding demonstrations, showing their anger and frustration by splashing paint on buildings and sidewalks and by breaking traffic signals. A few months later, when I met a Swiss businessman, I brought this up, telling him how surprised I was to hear something like that. I asked him why the youth of his country, who had every advantage in life, would riot and cause such damage? He thought the main reason was that the youth did not have anything to do, felt worthless, and that causing damage was their only means of showing their frustrations and gaining a sense of accomplishment.

Governments can help create an environment wherein people feel they are contributing to the welfare of their society. Now, with all kinds of environmental pollution, one national task could be to clean and restore the environment to its original beauty and dignity. Another national task could be to help the sick, poor, and discouraged people, first in one's own country, and then in other countries.

Some people become terribly depressed, even physically sick, after they retire. For thirty years or so, they go to work, accomplish something, and feel good about themselves. After retirement, all of a sudden they don't have anything to do and they feel worthless. Many others become involved in fulfilling activities and service after retirement. The extent of such activities may be so high that many people look forward to retiring for the express purpose of becoming involved in them.

In a family gathering where there were several middle-aged people talking about their company retirement policies and how they were looking forward to their retirements, a little boy sat with his grandmother, listening to the conversation very intently. After a while and in order to change the topic of the conversation, one of the men asked the boy what he wanted to be when he grew up. The little boy replied, "Retired."

Dr. Myers (1) summarizes the finding of many researchers, with respect to the acquisition of happiness due to accomplishment, as follows:

"Happiness is not the result of being rich, but a temporary consequence of having recently become richer. Better than a high income is a rising income. If we get a pay raise, receive an improved test grade, or bring home a promotion, we feel an initial surge of pleasure. But if these new realities continue, we adapt. So it happens that luxuries become necessities. If you are headed for the top, the pleasure of going by stairway will outlast that of a fast elevator ride."

Dr. Myers continues:

"Pleasure is always contingent upon change, and disappears with continuous satisfaction. Our very human tendency to adapt to new circumstances explains why. Despite the elation of triumph and the anguish of tragedy, even million-dollar lottery winners and paraplegics eventually return to variations of moment-to-moment happiness. People are unhappiest when they are alone and nothing needs doing."

When our work becomes our hobby and our accomplishments become our creations, they give us a greater sense of personal worth, freedom, and personal identity. Think of the great achievers such as Edison (with over 1,000 patents) and Mozart (with 600 compositions), who drew a great deal of joy from their accomplishments.

A note of caution here concerning accomplishment—it is true that we draw pleasure and joy from accomplishing something, but we should take great care not to become arrogant. In the Happinometry equation, you will recall that accomplishment was in the positive category, contributing to happiness. On the other hand, arrogance, jealousy, hate, hypocrisy, and so on, which may arise in the process of achieving something, are detractors from happiness. To eliminate these miseries, we must acknowledge that our accomplishments were made possible by the contributions of our big Partner, the Universe. (See Chapter 5.) Ideally, when we accomplish something, we are grateful to the Universe, our Partner, for having provided for all our needs and for having given us the ability to achieve what we did. This humility eliminates arrogance and other negative elements of happiness. If we become more arrogant, more jealous of others (who may have been more recognized or appreciated by our supervisors or the public), more hateful of our competitors, and so on, accomplishment as a whole may have done more harm than good in increasing our happiness.

It has been my practice to announce my students' grades, in a confidential manner, before reporting them to the registrar. About 20 years ago, four students, including two women, in my course of thermodynamics, had received the grade A in the course. Numerically their grades ranged between 90 to 98, so all received "A." Generally, after posting a class grade, many students come either to see their papers or to ask for a better grade. This time I was surprised to see the top student in the class coming to see me, not about her grade, but about another student's grade which was also an A. She argued that this other student, also a woman, who had only 90 points, as compared to her 98, should not have been given the same grade. I told her that in our system of grading, anything between 90 and 100 is translated into the letter grade A, and that I could not lower the other student's grade. Instead of being happy for her own accomplishment, this student was miserable. She was simply jealous of another student who had received the same reward.

For many people who have reached the highest plateau of happiness in giving love and rendering unconditional service, the joy derived from recognition is minimal. (See the Happinometry equation presented in Chapter 4.) In fact, they may not desire such recognition at all, believing that such acts may soften the intensity of their selfless service. For others, myself included, being recognized for achievements brings joy. As one learns to perform more unconditional and selfless acts of service, the need to be recognized by one's superiors or the public diminishes. However, in a work place, it becomes the duty of management to recognize the accomplishments of its employees without bias.

Contentment

Contentment is the state of being satisfied with who we are and what we have. This human quality may be more difficult to attain than it sounds, but the ability to be content at all times can be a major factor in bringing joy and happiness to life.

Discontentment is a rampant and widespread illness in the society; it shows up habitually in people's speech. Because of this habit, it has become very easy to air one's complaints and to discuss one's discontents, often to those in one's own families, to the closest co-workers, or even to complete strangers in order to strike up a conversation.

Complaining undermines contentment, not only for oneself, but for all beings in one's environment. Discontentment leads to uncontrolled desires and to excessive consumerism and wasteful-ness. Think of all the billions of dollars spent in the industrialized countries on advertising, creating discontentment, desires, con-sumerism, and wastefulness.

We need to make the most diligent efforts towards reducing our desires and wants and fostering contentment. In the case of chronic complaining, we can make great strides towards content-ment simply by developing the skill of keeping silent.

We can make every effort to cultivate contentment in our-selves by enumerating and appreciating what we have and who we are. If we want to bring a change, we work to bring it about, but in the mean time, dwell on all the things we have, and be contented because of them.

An American nurse working in a remote village in Nigeria once made an observation about a group of five-to-seven-year-old village boys playing in her driveway. She noticed that they had spent several hours engineering a toy truck from tin cans from the trash, and were pushing it with a stick with much delight and contentment. In the meantime, her own son who owned a huge toy truck in his room was looking on with envy.

In the following chapter, we consider education in human values, and suggest a method to cultivate these values. Contentment is one human quality which we need to work on and cultivate. I invite you to follow the method outlined in that chapter, making a diligent effort to foster this human quality, and experience the joy and happiness it brings.

Forgiveness

Chapter 3 made a brief mention of a case showing how a divorced woman who had lost custody of her children became cured of her sleeping problem, through the process of forgiving her ex-husband. Here is the full case.

Using forgiveness to heal a sleeping problem. In early 1987, I attended a national conference in Scottsdale, Arizona, on Research Into Enlightenment. The local organizers of the conference were a husband-wife team of medical doctors who believed in and practiced holistic treatment of patients. There were many case studies presented by medical doctors and psychologists at this conference. One case in particular has stayed with me all these years, and it involved a woman in her thirties who suffered from insomnia. She had gone through a terrible divorce about a year previously. Since she had also lost the custody of her three young children to her ex-husband in a bitter court battle, she was miserable. Her major problem was that each night, she fell asleep and dreamed of her ex-husband trying to kill her children with daggers. She would jump up from sleep and not be able to fall asleep again. She had consulted several physicians and had tried all kinds of medications without any effect. She then came to see Dr. McG. for treatment. Dr. McG., who presented this case at the conference, thought that no drug could cure her, and that she needed to use a different approach entirely. After much thought, she suggested forgiveness to her patient as the only way out of her predicament. At first, the patient objected that it would be impossible for her to forgive the man who had deliberately hurt her so much, but the doctor repeated her belief that there was no other way out except this. So, she worked with her patient for about six months, until the woman was finally able to forgive her ex-husband. After this, the patient was able to sleep comfortably.

What followed is even more interesting. A couple of months after the woman was successful in forgiving and releasing her ex-husband, he called on her and wanted to see her. The man had realized how he had done a terrible wrong to take the children from her (or perhaps the children bothered him too much, and he could not handle them). He came to apologize for all the pains he had inflicted on her; he was truly sorry for what he had done and asked for her forgiveness. She told him that she had already forgiven him. After a while, he begged her to marry him again.

It is amazing to note that forgiveness can not only cure a physical illness, but can also solve many other emotional problems. This woman could have spent a lot of money (if she had the resources) fighting her ex-husband in court and perhaps succeeding in regaining the custody of her children, all the while suffering from insomnia. After all, that is the way things are generally done these days: fight to get what you want. However, with the tireless encouragement of her counselor, she chose to forgive and release her ex-husband instead. The Universe, with all its wisdom and grace, started to work on her ex-husband, making him realize that he had made a terrible mistake and giving him the courage to come to her and apologize.

Forgiveness does more than just heal the physical body. When we forgive someone, or a situation, we release him, her, or it, to the Universe to be taken care of in the best way possible. We free ourselves of the burden of "prosecution," and feel relieved by this. We acknowledge that our big Partner, the Universe, knows best how to handle the particular case. In making such a release to the

Universe, we do not "instruct" it how to proceed. That is, we release any grudges we might hold against a person or situation. We simply let go of whatever we felt was our compromised right or damaged pride, and leave it to the Universe to handle with its grace and love for both ourselves and the other person or situation. Our reward for this action is the joy that we gain by forgiving and releasing the heavy weight of resentment.

I am not advocating complacency. We must use our best judgment in viewing what actions are appropriate for all concerned, particularly the person who has committed an error. We must realize that this person acted as best he or she knew how in seeking happiness, and only because of his or her ignorance did he or she cause harm to others. If we can realize that this person needs to be educated, we might see that love and forgiveness are some of the best means of educating anyone to give up his or her bad actions. We can then use our discrimination in finding out the best steps to take under any given circumstances. If our best judgment is to take legal steps against someone who has committed an error, this can then be accomplished without feelings of revenge and hatred.

The importance of forgiveness is in no place felt more than at home, between married couples. Almost all marriages start with love. Then, after a few years, for many couples love fades away, and the couple file for divorce. Many divorces might be prevented if the couple exercised more forgiveness. In all cases, forgiveness can foster and restore love between couples and within families.

Gratitude and Thanksgiving

I have had the good fortune of meeting and being associated with several people who are very happy and who constantly express their gratitude to the Universe. I have noted that in their daily activities, in doing their work, in meeting anyone, and in all their accomplishments, they realize that all these have been possible because of the generosity of the Universe. The life-supporting nature of planet Earth, along with the natural laws governing the behavior of materials and systems, and man's ability to learn about these laws and put them to use, have all made it possible for people to have food, clothing, shelter, health care, and today's modern conveniences. These people choose to express their thanks and gratitude to this generous and abundant Universe of ours, and to enjoy giving thanks. The Universe, upon receiving their gratitude and appreciation, increases its bounty and provides even more for them, specifically, more joy and happiness.

I have a confession to make—I love to give thanks! Perhaps more than any one other activity, I get a great deal of happiness each day from going about giving thanks for everything I encounter.

During the day I do not lose touch with the idea of expressing my gratitude to the Universe, but particularly at night, I set aside special moments for this purpose. During this time, I usually visualize and enumerate all that the Universe has given me: my health, my accomplishments, all the conveniences, the people in my life, and so on. I acknowledge the marvelous ways that nature functions to sustain my life, as well as the lives and well-being of billions upon billions of living beings on the planet. I choose to give thanks to the Universe for all of these. I never forget the role that the Universe plays as my big Partner in my efforts.

In expressing my gratitude and thanks to the Universe, I often remember to thank the people who have helped bring about the things that I enjoy. I thank them personally if possible or, if not, I thank them mentally. Being aware of all the conveniences that we have today—electricity, central heating and air conditioning, healthy food, cooking facilities, telephones, radio, television, automobile, computers, and much more—I can't help but thank all those men and women whose efforts helped bring about all of these conveniences, the people who, except for the few who are remembered because of their discoveries or inventions, are mostly unknown. They are thanked because, without their efforts, humankind would not be enjoying all of these conveniences.

During meal times, I make every effort to be quiet, first thanking all those hands that helped to provide the meal, then visualizing how different organs of my body function to assimilate the food and provide nourishment. By this act, I enjoy my meal more, and I am sure I help improve its digestion. I always thank all those present who worked to prepare the meal. This, I am sure, gives them pleasure and joy too. The meals are always tastier when consumed by loving and appreciative attitudes and when prepared by loving and caring persons. No wonder everyone talks about how delicious his mother's cooking is! I am sure the love that pours out or emanates from the mother while cooking, while thinking with love of her family, affects the cooking process and helps to bring out the best taste in the food. After all, preparing a meal is not just adding water and heat to food items according to a set of instructions for making them edible. There is an art to cooking and preparing a meal. The state of the mind, particularly the love emanating from the cook and all those working in the kitchen, adds to the taste and nutritional value of the meal. I have not seen any scientific proof for this statement, but I have no doubt that this is so.

A mother, seeing her family appreciating her cooking and other efforts, becomes happier and will give more of herself and prepare the next meals with even greater love and enthusiasm. The Universe, or Mother Nature, is the same. When we appreciate the Universe for its efforts in sustaining us, we cause it to provide even more.

I have been fortunate to have met people who often express a sense of gratitude for what they have. My mother is one of these people. Literally one out of every four words that she speaks is an offering of thanks. Mrs. A.B., a distant relative of mine, a woman in her seventies, is nearly paralyzed in one arm. When I saw her a few years ago, she said she never thinks of this arm. Instead, she is thankful for the other arm, which functions properly. William Barclay, Scotland's scholar-writer, expressed in his later years, "I am almost completely deaf. But this means I can sleep without trouble in a noisy hotel by a railway station. And I can concentrate far better on work and study, for I have no distractions. . . . A handicap has its compensations."

Thus, one can turn a lack or deficiency into an asset. For everything we feel is lacking in our lives, tens or hundreds of good things abound. It is up to us: we can choose to think of lack and be miserable, or choose to be grateful and happy for the things that we have.

Mr. J.G., a man in his thirties, was one who had chosen to be grateful for what he had. I met this young man several years ago when I was in the process of changing my residence. On one occasion, when I had planned to take a taxi to the airport, he volunteered to take me. During the ride, I learned a lot from him and enjoyed listening to him. He constantly expressed his gratitude for all he had. In fact, he kept saying how he had everything that a man could ever hope to have—a lovely wife and three children, employment as a firefighter in a petrochemical company, and odd jobs during his off periods to supplement his income. For these odd jobs he never demanded a fee. He simply told the people, "You pay me whatever you want; I accept it with gratitude and will never say anything." He lived very modestly, but was happy and joyous. He said his salary from the company met only his family's basic needs and that, with earnings from his odd jobs, he could buy some of the other things they needed. He later showed me some things he had bought to take home that day. He said they were all needed by his children and wife, and were surprises for them. He felt great for having worked and accomplished something, and his family anticipated his returning home and receiving unexpected gifts. They all had fun and were very happy.

After he let me off at the airport, I tried to visualize the lifestyle of this young man. What I saw was a life full of love, contentment, and happiness. He and his family had a very modest lifestyle, but they were constantly appreciative and grateful for what they had. He was one who looked at life as a game, and who played it with joy and constant thanksgiving. I was happy when I rode with this joyous man for about thirty minutes nearly six years ago. I feel joy even now thinking about him and in sharing my experience of meeting him. It is amazing how just thinking of a happy person can bring happiness inside.

Exercise 14: *Write down all of the things in your life for which you are grateful to the Universe. Start with your physical health, your family and their health, all of the conveniences you are enjoying in your life, all of the people in your life who have helped you become who you are, and so on. Make a complete list and post it on your mirror, or wherever you can see it often. Anytime you feel down about anything, go back and look at this list, and be thankful for what you have.*

Hope

Hope is the quality of life that makes us look forward to a better tomorrow. Hope is an expectation for success and a better future; hope is having something to live for. Hope is hearing the melody and the song of future. When there is hope in the heart and mind, there is joy and happiness in life.

Some people, particularly those in poverty, may have lost hope and see nothing in their future. Many crimes and suicides are committed by hopeless people because they feel there is nothing more for them to do or accomplish. These people have no hope for a better tomorrow. This can be eliminated if they can learn to trust the Universe.

Everyone's life has gloomy times, but this is no reason to become hopeless. One can develop a positive attitude and view all events as learning opportunities. Then, by taking the first step and doing one's share of work, by being patient and trusting, the Universe, the big Partner in life, will do the rest and provide.

A valuable service project for each individual or community would be to talk to people who have temporarily lost hope. This service includes giving them love, nurturing, and assistance in finding ways to get their lives back together and to feel useful again. Governments can also help generate hope by devising national and international plans that involve people, particularly the young.

Optimism and Well-wishfulness

Being optimistic and wishing well to all are means of acquiring instant joy.

We need to develop the attitude of looking for the "good" things in life. I believe that every event is a lesson in the University of Life and is therefore appropriate for all those concerned. Only by my limited knowledge and awareness of the grand scheme of things can I call some things good, and other things bad. In reality, everything is right.

We may be upset about some people or a situation. It has become part of our nature that when we think of these people or situations, we automatically remember the "bad" or the "terrible" acts which were committed, or the harsh words which were said. While it may be impossible to put such deeds completely out of our awareness, it is quite possible, through some practice, to keep them from dominating our minds and thoughts. We can try to identify the positive or "good" elements of those people or situations, and dwell on those. If this is still impossible, then we should make every effort to direct our minds to whatever is good, loving, and beautiful to us. I know it is very difficult to put the thought of a terrible act out of our minds, but we should make an earnest effort to achieve it. This is for our own sake, for our own joy, and for our own health. Louise Hay (2) has discovered that most of our physical problems or sicknesses result from negative emotional states that have prevailed for years, particularly pessimism, or seeing "bad things" in people and situations. As I mentioned earlier, we should be aware of the situation, but choose to view only positive or good things in it.

Master Teacher Jesus was once walking with His disciples when they ran into the decomposed carcass of a dog. All of the disciples complained about the terrible smell of the decaying body. Jesus told them, "But look at its beautiful white teeth."

In all situations we face, we can either become annoyed by them, or develop a positive attitude and think of their positive merits. Again, I am not advocating complacency here—far from it. If we feel we need to do something about a situation, we should do it by all means, but should not develop any hatred in our heart for anyone or anything. We should not allow our minds to be occupied by the things which we consider to be "bad." We should consider all events as lessons that we, as well as many others, need to learn in our pursuit of happiness. For the joy of it, we need always be an optimist.

Optimism plays an important role in our physical well-being. Dr. Myers (1), in reviewing the studies carried out by many researchers, concludes that:

> "In general, optimistic people are less bothered by various illnesses and recover better from coronary bypass surgery and cancer. Blood tests provide a reason, by linking optimism with stronger immune defenses. Optimists also enjoy greater success. Rather than seeing setbacks as signs of their incompetence, they view them as flukes or as suggesting a new approach."

Another method of acquiring instant joy is to wish people, things, or situations well. When I was teaching at Arizona State University several years ago, I used to ride my bicycle to work every day. It used to take about 20 minutes from my home to the university, but the route was quiet and the ride very pleasant. Furthermore, I used to leave home very early in the morning, when the weather was cool, the streets quiet, and the birds very active. It was such a delight to hear and see the birds, particularly the hummingbirds, flying around feeding, or simply singing and chasing each other. Any time that I saw a car going by, or a person walking, I simply wished that person well. I didn't know anyone, but looking at the person, I wished him or her well. By the time I arrived at my office I was filled with joy and energy, and I taught my classes with more enthusiasm. By simply wishing well to people whom I did not know at all, I acquired instant joy and happiness.

It has become my practice to do this well-wishing as much as possible when I am on the street. Now, in Southern California, where I either walk or ride my bicycle to work (not too many people living in the Los Angeles area are as lucky as I am to live so close to their place of work), I do the same thing. I make every effort to wish well to every person, every bird, or every flower and plant that I see. When I pass by a house where the owners have maintained a nice lawn, beautiful flowers or shrubs, or even a neat building, I simply wish them well. I enjoy seeing these beautiful things, and I ask the Universe to grant happiness to the people responsible for them. The result of this seemingly "weird" act is my own joy.

This instant joy and happiness can be enhanced even more if we consider the people who have "harmed" us and wish them well too. This is very hard to do, but well worth the effort, with the great joy of forgiveness as its reward.

Exercise 15: *List the names of those people whom you believe have inflicted pains on you, or who have caused you to suffer. If you can, obtain their pictures and have them handy. Now, consider one of these people, and look at his or her picture. Then sit down in a quiet spot, close your eyes, take several deep breaths, and visualize that person as sitting directly in front of you. Mentally, reach for and hold his or her hands and, while looking at his or her eyes, mentally say, "I know you have done a great deal of harm to me and have caused a great deal of anguish in my life, but now I release and forgive you, and wish you well for all that you need to do during the rest of your life." Mentally repeat the second half of this last sentence several times. As an effective supplement to this process, I suggest you record this affirmation. With soft background music, while you have relaxed yourself completely, repeat the above statement aloud, repeating the statement of forgiveness and well-wishfulness several times. You may then listen to your own voice several times during the day, particularly at night before you go to sleep. Try to fall asleep with this soft background music and your own affirmation of forgiving and well-wishing for the person who has done you harm. In both your mental affirmation and during the recording of it, feel compassion toward this person, believing that he or she did not know any better.*

Carry out this process as often as you can, for one person at a time, until you are completely healed and have been able to forgive this person and wish well for him or her. Do not demand or expect any apologies from these people. If it comes later, accept it with gratitude, but do not demand it as a prerequisite for your well-wishing and forgiveness. Allow yourself to feel joy during and immediately after this process. Carry out the same well-wishfulness process for all others who have caused you harm.

Respect and Reverence for the Environment and for All Life Forms

A sign and an outcome of love is the respect and reverence we develop toward all beings. When you are in love, you simply love, revere, and respect anything and everything. It is impossible to do otherwise.

It is estimated that for every human living on this planet, about 100 million beings exist in the animal kingdom. The Universe, in its generosity and abundance, provides for all of them, as well as for all of us. We have no right to infringe on their rights of existence and well-being. That is, we should respect their right to make use of natural resources for their sustenance and habitation, and realize the fact that we are all sharing the same planet. We realize that their rates of consumption of resources are basically very small, with very few environmental disruptions. Furthermore, we appreciate that each animal plays a unique and important role in maintaining the ecosystem.

It is heartening to see an environmental revolution taking place now. Every day more and more people become concerned about environmental protection, not just for human sustenance, but also for the well-being of other species.

Respect and reverence for other beings adds to our happiness and joy. In a sense it provides us with a certain feeling of appreciation and gratitude to the Universe for being the way it is. When I look at a tree, a flower, a bird, or the pictures of a deer, a lion, and so on, I can't help but marvel at each one's beauty, magnificence, talent, and the role that it plays in maintaining the equilibrium of the planet. It gives me a great deal of joy anytime I see, read, or think about these beings. I become awestruck with the magnificence, splendor, and beauty of the Universe. The Universe, which has so marvelously designed these and all beings on this planet, takes care of them and sustains them. I am a being on this planet too; it is therefore going to sustain me, as it has so far. Not only has the Universe sustained and met my needs, but it has done so for millions of years for all the estimated 100 billion people who have lived on this planet. I accept this generosity and the ability of the Universe in faith. There is, therefore, no need for me to worry about anything or expect anything from anybody. Along with this faith, I develop respect, love, and reverence for all beings, and do everything within my power to make sure that they too are happy sharing the natural resources of the planet with me.

Plants and animals are happy when their environment and habitat are left clean, pure, undisturbed, and unpolluted. It is such a joy to see healthy and happy plants and animals. As a sign of respect and reverence toward Nature, I need to cut down wasting what I use. I know that wastage or overconsumption of any material or energy eventually harms and damages the environment.

Modest Living

Many people consider the average lives of North Americans to be extravagant and excessive, with their large homes, appliances, automobiles, and all of today's living conveniences. This extravagant living, along with excessive use of private automobiles for traveling to and from work, and a lack of concern about the use of materials and energy in everyday life, has resulted in the fact that the United States, with less than 6% of the world's population, uses about 30% of the world's natural resources. This lifestyle of overconsumption has caused a great deal of air, water, and land pollution in the country, and has helped greatly to degrade the environment throughout the world. It is only when you travel to other countries, particularly to the developing ones, that you realize how wastefully North Americans live. Here are a few extreme examples:

I rented a three-bedroom house in Phoenix, Arizona, in the summer of 1975, but, as you will see shortly, lived in it for only one month. The house was built very poorly, with no concern toward energy conservation. It was equipped with three large air conditioners that ran all day long to keep the indoor temperature comfortable during the hot Phoenix weather. Even though the unit cost of electricity was very low, these air conditioners used enough electricity to raise the electric bill to a level equal to the monthly house rent. This made me move quickly from this house into an apartment, where the cost of electricity was only about 20% of the rent.

Here is another story about the energy unconsciousness of some people. An old couple who moved to Phoenix, Arizona, from New England, missed their fireplace. However, the weather was not cold enough to warrant using one. The few days in winter when they could use the fireplace to heat the house just weren't enough. So, they decided to set the air-conditioner's thermostat low enough to keep the house really cold. Then they used the fireplace to enjoy its heat.

Such lifestyles are more than extravagant; they are plain wasteful. You see the same excessiveness and wastefulness in food consumption, in the packaging of food and other materials, and in almost everything used in North America. Since we are concerned about increasing our happiness, we need to see whether our lifestyle actually contributes to happiness or not. Going back to the Happinometry equation, $(H = J - F - E)$, and all the terms constituting J, F, and E (see Chapter 4), we note that the only place that our material lifestyle can contribute to H is in accomplishment, where adding to our material belongings contributes to the feeling of having accomplished something. However taken to excess, this can have several negative side effects. One of the side effects of excessive material consumption is harm to the environment. Other side effects that generally accompany wealth include jealousy, worry, attachment, arrogance, and so on. (You will recall that these terms appear in the misery category, E.) That is, when rating our happiness in the Happinometry tables, we may be able to give ourselves a grade of 4 for accomplishment, but we may also have to give ourselves grades 4 for the growth of worry, attachment, and any of the other misery items mentioned above that our material accomplishment may bring. As the result, we may very well end up with a much lower value for H. A wiser approach would be to mindfully cut down on wastes, accept a more modest lifestyle, and spend our additional income in helping eradicate the indignities of joblessness, hunger, and homelessness, or in restoring the environment to its original beauty and purity. In short, to increase our happiness, it is more logical to be concerned about the well-being of our society and environment than paying more attention to our own material wealth. I am sure you agree with me that we can live very comfortably and be joyous while having a very modest lifestyle.

Cutting down on waste. I am delighted to see that as a part of the on-going environmental revolution, there is a growing concern and consciousness about the conservation of materials and energy. Nonetheless, we need to be more than just conscious and concerned; we need to take action—cut down on wastage, place a ceiling on our desires, and live modestly.

Modest living is difficult to define. I know it is different at different times and in different countries. Everyone must decide for himself if he is living modestly or not. Once we have changed our attitudes and accepted the practice of acquiring happiness through means other than wealth, fame and social position, it will not be difficult to make a proper choice of lifestyle. It will not be hard for loving and concerned persons to decide how they want to conduct the material aspects of life. Seeing homeless and jobless people in their own neighborhoods, seeing starving and dying children in Africa on television, or reading about suffering people (or animals) somewhere else in the world, people will feel compassion toward them and decide to help reduce their miseries.

Once compassion and love are fostered in people's hearts, it will not be so difficult for people to decide what to do in life. It will be easy to decide which actions will bring more joy—moving to a larger and more expensive residence, exchanging a car for a newer model, buying a newer or a larger television and so on, or saving money to help feed the hungry and shelter the homeless. It will become easy to discern between adding more to one's living conveniences, or helping find cures to life-threatening diseases such as cancer, AIDS, and so on. If compassion and love are foremost in the heart, people will be more than willing to help eradicate diseases and the indignities of joblessness and homelessness. People will take all necessary actions to help teach human values to our young (and old) people.

Helping to restore the dignity of others in securing jobs so as to feed and shelter themselves and their families, along with helping to eliminate other physical and emotional suffering, are means of rendering SERVICE—the most effective way of attaining joy and happiness in life.

In addition, one of the most important steps we can take in securing a modest living is to cut down, and finally eliminate, the wasting of money, food and other materials, time, and energy. It is hard to change a lifestyle that we are used to. But can we make changes in our lifestyle, live modestly, and be equally comfortable? You might be amazed at how it is possible to get used to almost any lifestyle and have equal physical comfort. Let me share with you the following example to illustrate how it is possible to have a comfortable sleep under the harshest of conditions.

My trips to India have all been very interesting and educational. I have seen many people who slept on the street (thanks to the warm weather of the country) with nothing under or over them. But the strangest sight of all was what I saw when traveling by bus from Bombay to Bangalore in January of 1990. It was a tiring 24-hour-long journey. When evening came, I saw a young man simply lie down on the bus floor and go to sleep. He did not use any blankets, sheets, pillows or anything. He was not even concerned about getting his clothes dirty. He thought it was better to have a good rest by lying down, than to try snoozing while sitting up like the rest of the passengers. Did he fall asleep? I am sure he did. A couple of times during the night, when the bus stopped at roadside restaurants for passengers to get off and stretch or eat something, other passengers had to awaken this young man to let them pass.

This was indeed very surprising to me. When I travel and need to sleep in different beds, I always have difficulty adjusting to the new conditions (particularly the firmness of the pillow) and sleeping comfortably. But here was a young Indian man, with nothing under his head or his body, sleeping apparently comfortably on the very rough floor of a bus, which was moving at high speeds on rough and bumpy roads. I am sure he was not used to having any bedding for a comfortable sleep. The only difficulty he needed to overcome, I believe, was the rough floor and the bumpy road. And he succeeded in accomplishing that easily.

Placing a ceiling on our desires. I shared the above example with you, not because I wish to advocate poverty or harsh living, nor do I condemn the use of modern-day conveniences. In fact, we cannot have a static lifestyle. New discoveries and inventions are made constantly which bring us even more conveniences, and these have positive value to society. The point is that we need to limit our desires as to how far we want to go in acquiring all the available conveniences. It is important that we do not become attached to them, as attachment is a negative element in the Happinometry equation.

By citing the above extreme example, I wish to emphasize that: *1) our lifestyle, beyond the minimum needed for physical comfort, does not guarantee us any happiness; and 2) we should not be so attached to our belongings that we cannot live without them.*

This is to suggest that, by limiting our desires, we not be so overly concerned about bodily needs and sense pleasures. As mentioned earlier, we need to keep our bodies healthy and well so that we can proceed more effectively towards acquiring happiness and be better able to express unconditional love by rendering unconditional service. This goal is aided by having clean and comfortable clothing and shelter, and modern, but modest, living conveniences. However, our well-being is tied to the welfare and well-being of all people and beings. We need to be concerned about them, too. Remember, the happiness and welfare of all beings affects our own in return.

By living extravagantly, by using more than we need, and particularly by wasting materials and energy, we create environmental pollution that harms everyone, including ourselves. Let me emphasize again that we can acquire the greatest happiness through sharing, giving, and serving, and not through accumulating wealth and living extravagantly.

We are here on this planet to be happy. Living modestly, cutting down on wastage of money, food, time, and energy, and using our extra time and money to help others, are small prices to pay for the acquisition of lasting and widespread joy and happiness. Let us expand our horizons to include the welfare and comfort of all beings, not just our own. Only through these attitudes and actions can we secure happiness and an everlasting and **sustainable, joyous society.**

Exercise 16. *Review your lifestyle and list the areas in which you can cut down on wastes. I urge you to experiment and to prove this principle for yourself—you have only happiness to gain! Estimate the monetary value of these savings, and list what you can do with it towards increasing happiness.*

10

THE IMPORTANCE OF
CULTIVATING HUMAN VALUES

*If you want to be continuously victorious over your problems,
study and resolutely master each (human) value:
Integrity, courage, enthusiasm, happiness, faith, hope, love,
and make them part of your life. You will achieve success
beyond anything you have ever experienced before.*

—Norman Vincent Peale

You will recall our Happinometry equation, $(H = J - F - E)$, where H stands for happiness. So far, our discussion has been limited to what each one of us can do individually to increase his or her happiness. This and the following chapters are devoted to what we can do individually and collectively as a society to increase happiness. This chapter deals specifically with increasing the elements of joy, (J) in the Happinometry equation, and with eliminating the emotional miseries, (E) in that equation, under the heading of education in human values. Reduction of the miseries due to sickness and physical discomfort (F), will be discussed in the following chapter.

Education in human values is a means that each one of us can employ for the benefit of increasing happiness. As individuals, we can learn to implement human values in our daily lives. As a group, we can make every effort to teach and foster these values in our children and youth.

Happiness is an inside job; we acquire it chiefly through our own individual efforts. No one can cause more joy in our lives than ourselves through our own endeavor. However, the welfare and joy of other beings, including the environment, directly affects our own happiness. We therefore need to be concerned about them, particularly the happiness and well-being of other human beings. So, for our own sake, we need to help others to attain happiness. Our love has to encompass all beings, not just the few who may be in our lives or in our immediate surroundings. Furthermore, helping other people acquire joy and happiness is a pure form of service. To maximize efforts in rendering the most effective service, we may find it necessary to pool our resources and work together.

Individually, our concern is to maximize our lifetime happiness. Similarly, a society's or a country's concern ought to be to maximize its happiness. That is, the efforts of a country should be directed toward maximizing its National Index of Happiness, or NIH. (See Chapter 4.) This includes all activities of the society or country, including the economy, education, health care, research, foreign affairs, and so on.

The most important effort of a society, I believe, is investing for its future, investing for its children and youth and making sure that they can acquire their birthright of happiness. Much of this investment takes place, rightly, in conventional education, where the future generation learns how to make its living. Even more important than career-training efforts, however, is education in human values. Human values training could be the best possible preventive effort in reducing elements of misery, in eliminating crimes and other social diseases, and, further, in maintaining the health of the future generation.

The following story, the "Parable of the Dangerous Cliff," (5) describes the essence of this assertion.

'Twas a dangerous cliff, as they freely confessed.
    Though to walk near its crest was so pleasant;
But over its terrible edge there had slipped
    A duke, and full many a peasant.
The people said something would have to be done,
    But their projects did not at all tally.
Some said, "Put a fence 'round the edge of the cliff,"
    Some, "An ambulance down in the valley."

The lament of the crowd was profound and was loud,
    As their hearts overflowed with their pity;
But the cry for the ambulance carried the day
    As it spread through the neighboring city.
A collection was made, to accumulate aid,
    And the dwellers in highway and alley
Gave dollars or cents—not to furnish a fence—
    But an ambulance down in the valley.

"For the cliff is all right if you're careful," they said;
    "and if folks ever slip and are dropping,
It isn't the slipping that hurts them so much
    As the shock down below—when they're stopping."
So for years (we have heard), as these mishaps occurred
    Quick forth would the rescuers sally,
To pick up the victims who fell from the cliff
    With the ambulance down in the valley.

Said one, to his plea, "It's a marvel to me
    That you'd give so much greater attention
To repairing results than to curing the cause;
    You had much better aim at prevention.
For the mischief, of course, should be stopped at its source.
    Come, neighbors and friends, let us rally.
It is far better sense to rely on a fence
    Than an ambulance down in the valley."

"He is wrong in his head," the majority said;
    "He would end all our earnest endeavor.
He's a man who would shirk this responsible work,
    But we will support it forever.
Aren't we picking up all, just as fast as they fall,
    And giving them care liberally?
A superfluous fence is of no consequence,
    If the ambulance works in the valley."

The story looks queer as we've written it here,
    But things oft occur that are stranger.
More humane, we assert, than to succor the hurt,
    Is the plan of removing the danger.
The best possible course is to safeguard the source;
    Attend to things rationally
—Yes, build up the fence and let us dispense
    With the ambulance in the alley.

—Anonymous

Much can be done by a society to prevent future mishaps, and at much lower costs, than treating the symptoms.

Exercise 17. *List ideas as to what your community can do to increase the happiness of all its members. Then list what you think state and federal governments can do to increase the State Index of Happiness (SIH) and the National Index of Happiness (NIH.)*

Significance of Education in Human Values *

Fundamental to any future achievement, accomplishment, and progress of a society is the education it offers its children and

---

* A great portion of the material presented here is derived from the teaching of Sri Sathya Sai Baba (6-8), whose educational system, in India, from primary school to doctoral programs, teaches and exemplifies the Human Values proposed by Him (8).

youth. These days, the aim of nearly all educational systems throughout the world is to prepare the youth for making a living and surviving the storms which often arise in today's world economy. While it is necessary to have a skill and to know a profession in order to meet physical needs and live comfortably, by no means is such an effort sufficient. *More important than this education on how to make a living is the education on how to truly live, how to be happy.* It is extremely important for educators, themselves, in conjunction with parents and all figures of authority to teach and exemplify the human values. Societies now make huge investments in fighting crimes, in taking care of the symptoms of a dire social predicament. Any and all investment in human values education will prove well worth the effort and, in the long run, will more than pay for itself.

Description of the Human Values

There are many human qualities that can be classified under the broad term of human values. Norman Vincent Peale considers the following seven qualities to be the values to live by: Integrity, Courage, Enthusiasm, Happiness, Faith, Hope, and Love. (9) Dr. Peale explains:

"You must make a commitment to learn them and use them. They are not easy, but by committing yourself to learning them and living them, you will acquire the basis for becoming a great person. When you get discouraged, when you cannot seem to make it, there is one thing you must practice. It is that priceless ingredient of success: relentless effort. Never give up; never quit." (9)

Sri Sathya Sai Baba considers the following five characteristics as constituting the human values (6,7):

Truth, Righteousness, Peace, Love and Non-violence, whose respective Sanskrit names are: *Sathya, Dharma, Shanti, Prema,* and *Ahimsa.*

Vinayak K. Gokak, the late Vice Chancellor of the Sri Sathya
Sai Institute of Higher Learning, elaborates on these five human
values as follows (7):

"When we speak about Human Values, we enumerate five
principal values which we have taken from Sathya Sai Baba's
teachings; they are the key words for the philosophy of life. The first
one is Sathya (Truth). Now there are two ways in which truth can
be spoken of. There is intellectually ascertainable truth based on
science, intellect and reason. There is another understanding which
does not come out of reason, but of a true mystical intuition. . . . In
a flash of glorious perception, you realize truth."

"Next comes Dharma (Righteousness). It is concerned with
what we do—engaging in right action. Here the human will is
involved. If I train my will to do things correctly and exercise it in
the proper manner, then I can be confident that I will end up doing
things correctly. Dharma (Righteousness) is training my will. Will
is something totally different from desire; sometimes we misunder-
stand the function of these faculties....Will is akin to intuition, the
exercise of will results in certainty of right action; unless the will is
deviated from its path by desire or other impulses, it will act in the
correct way. This is Dharma, right action."

"Shanti is the inner peace and stands for the training of the heart
where we attain an equipoise and become a balanced personality. It
is there within the depths of one's personality that one attains this
peace and knows how to control one's emotions. This is a necessary
part of education, for what is the good of leaving people intellectually well-trained but wild and almost primitive in their emotions?
They will be lopsided personalities. Shanti trains one to gain balance
and stability in one's emotions."

Dr. Gokak continues:

"Now we come to Prema (Love) and Ahimsa (Non-violence),
the fourth and the fifth values which are based on the soul and the
spirit. The love, which is the universal love, is the same as the
mystical intuition which has already been touched upon above. The

non-violence that is spoken of here also has a universal character. With this value of non-violence, we come to the social obligations of a human being. Once you have the right vision of truth, the right understanding and practice of the will, the right emotional balance and equipoise with yourself, then you begin to experience a release of the feeling of universal love. This can only come from a pure personality in which no emotional debris or wild impulses cover up these finer wellsprings. When the debris is cleared, the full expression of love arises spontaneously. It manifests itself in non-violence and in universal love toward all."

Dr. Gokak concludes:

"Human Values education means educating in these five values that have been discussed here. What we are doing now in most universities in the world is educating a person's intellect. There is a lot of stuffing of the brain with information; the students we are sending out go back the way they came, with the addition of some information, half of which is soon forgotten. They are not intellectually developed, their sensibilities have not matured, and deeper qualities are absent. But if we have Human Values education, then during the same time that is spent on other education, we can cultivate all the various components of the complete personality that we have been covering here. As teachers, if we are prepared to spend some time in understanding these Human Values and practicing them, we may be able to refine ourselves into very sensitive instruments who pass this on to the youngsters who sit before us in the classroom."

The above five human values, presented by Sri Sathya Sai Baba, encompass all of the human qualities. For purposes of discussion, let us break down those chief values into the following list of human qualities. The list is not meant to be exhaustive; there may be other values or qualities that you might consider to be important that do not appear in the list. If so, please write those down in the space provided. Consider these to be the values that we need to cultivate in ourselves and in our children and youth to help increase our own happiness, the happiness of society, and particularly that of the future generations.

To me, love is the most important human value to foster in ourselves and in our children and youth. Therefore, it appears first in the list. The rest of the qualities follow in alphabetical order.

Human Values

Love	Enthusiasm	Persistence
Acceptance	Forgiveness	Reverence for Nature
Ceiling on Desires	Gratitude	Sacrifice
Compassion	Humility	Self-Confidence
Contentment	Hope	Surrender
Conservation	Integrity	Tolerance
Courage	Linkage with a Master	Trust
Dedication	Moderation	Truth
Desire to Serve	Optimism	Unity
Detachment	Patience	Well-wishfullness
Devotion	Peace	___ ___ ___
___ ___ ___	___ ___ ___	

Most of the terms in the above list are self-explanatory. In Chapter 9, we briefly discussed a few of them, including placing a ceiling on desires, living modestly, and developing respect and reverence toward nature and all beings. I have listed the desire to serve unconditionally and selflessly as a human value. It needs to be fostered and emphasized as the equivalent of love, which we need to give to others in order to increase our lifetime happiness.

The importance of linkage with a Master was discussed in Chapter 8. In addition to the benefits enumerated there, this essential connection can be employed to foster the human values. (See Exercises 18 through 20.)

Research Into Cultivation of Human Values (RICH-Values)

There is a need for balanced education: to teach skills and professions for making a more comfortable living and, even more important, to foster and cultivate human values. While the former teaches how to make a living, the latter emphasizes how to live.

How to embark on education in human values is both beyond the scope of this book and the area of my expertise. There is a need for an extensive research program to determine the best and the most effective way of cultivating these values at different levels of the educational system. It needs to be broadly inclusive, from preschool through university education. It should also include the population at large, beyond those directly engaged in the school environments.

It is suggested that a center or an institute be founded at the state or federal levels for **Research Into Cultivation of Human Values (RICH-Values.)** This Center for RICH-Values needs sufficient funding to draw on the talents of those educated and gifted individuals who (1) are concerned about the causes of the problems facing today's society, (2) believe in education in human values, and (3) have the appropriate expertise in psychology, education, and other related areas of human development.

One thing is clear to me: human values can best be cultivated through example. We cannot foster human values simply by reading or talking about them. I believe the greatest of the human qualities is Love, Love translated into unconditional and selfless Service. We need to search for and find people who have such qualities. As these people render their services unconditionally, they do not seek fame and fanfare. As such, one needs to search to find them. In addition, the lifestyle of these people should be brought to the attention of all those for whom education in human values is intended. Their love for people and the services that these people have rendered (or are rendering) should be presented to students learning human values in the most interesting and enjoyable way, in the form of videos, books, interviews, and so on.

Education in human values is not a subject to be dealt with separately from other education. That is, we cannot have separate class sessions or hours set aside in the school curricula to teach these values, as we do for teaching sciences, foreign languages, and so on. The human values have to be cultivated in students as a part of all subjects. This can be done only by teachers who already possess and exemplify such values and qualities. Teachers are role models for students, and can be revered as symbols of the highest qualities by them. The society should provide financial rewards for these teachers to secure their comfortable living.

For those who intend to make education their career, it is essential that they possess utmost love for people in general, and for future school children in particular. As part of the teacher-training curricula, several community service projects should be devised in which student-teachers become directly involved. Their training should also include typical service projects in which their future students become involved and carry out.

As a further means of fostering human values, the life stories of people who have served lovingly without selfish expectations should be brought to the attention of children through books, videos, and any other appropriate manner. Such people should be continually venerated and honored for their work as society's greatest heroes, including naming buildings after them, providing scholarships in their names, and so on.

The Effect of Human Values in Eliminating Misery

Implementing the human values listed above can reduce our misery and increase our happiness. The cultivation of these values as a service to others helps the society to acquire joy and happiness, which contributes again to our own happiness. However, let us now consider which of these qualities has the greatest impact in eliminating a specific element of misery. Do they all have the same effect?

Referring again to the Happinometry equation, ($H = J - F - E$), we discussed that not all the elements constituting J, such as love, forgiveness, gratitude, hope, and so on, have the same weight in increasing J. The same thing applies to the qualities listed above as Human Values. Each one of these values has a different effect or impact in reducing each of the elements of misery that constitute E.

For example, fostering of the human quality "humility" has a tremendous effect towards eliminating the misery element of "arrogance." If we were to choose a number between 1 and 10 to represent this impact, with 10 being the highest and 1 the lowest effect, I would select the number 10 for the impact humility has in alleviating arrogance. If a person has attained the quality of humility, even for one moment, for that moment the element of arrogance will be completely absent. To make it easier to see how each human value has an impact on eliminating or reducing other elements of misery, I have constructed a table whereby each of us can contemplate and evaluate for ourselves these cross-related effects by assigning our own values from one to ten for each quality or human value as it affects each of the elements of misery. This "Misery Eradication, or Misery Elimination" table lists all the human values vertically and all elements of misery horizontally. The effect of any human quality on any element of misery can be assigned by a number, which can be printed in the box where the coordinates (qualities) meet.

With over thirty human values listed above and over forty misery elements (see Chapter 3, page 20), listing them all in one table is unwieldy. Therefore, we suggest breaking the complete table into one or more smaller ones, considering only a portion at a time of the human values and their opposing or related misery elements. In other words, perhaps it is easier to consider 10 human values and 20 related misery elements at a time and prepare several tables like it to account for all the cross-effects.

Table 5
Effect of Human Values in Eradicating the Elements of Misery

Select a number between 1 and 10 for each box that best determines the effect of the human value (listed across the top) on the misery element listed on the left. Leave the box blank if you see no effect between a particular human value and one or more misery elements.

MISERY ELEMENTS \ HUMAN VALUES	LOVE	CONTENTMENT	FORGIVENESS	GRATITUDE	HUMILITY	LINK W/MASTER	OPTIMISM	PATIENCE	TRUST	WELL-WISHFUL.
ANGER										
ANXIETY										
ARROGANCE										
ATTACHMENT										
CRITICISM										
DEPRESSION										
DESPAIR										
EXPECTATION										
FEAR										
GREED										
GUILT										
HATE										
JEALOUSY										
JUDGMENT										
POWERLESSNESS										
REJECTION										
RESENTMENT										
VENGEANCE										
WORRY										
WORTHLESSNESS										
TOTAL										

(Add all numbers in each column and write the result above.)

Table 5 is an example of such a "10/20" or "Misery Eradication" table. We have arbitrarily selected the following human values from the list suggested above:

Love	Linkage with Master
Contentment	Optimism
Forgiveness	Patience
Gratitude	Trust
Humility	Well-wishfulness

along with the following 20 misery elements:

Anger	Guilt
Anxiety	Hate
Arrogance	Jealousy
Attachment	Judgment
Criticism	Powerlessness
Depression	Rejection
Despair	Resentment
Expectation	Vengeance
Fear	Worry
Greed	Worthlessness.

Table 6 is a blank table for you to complete. First choose ten qualities from the list of human values, then up to twenty elements from the misery list given in Chapter 3 (page 20). Then follow the remaining steps described in Exercise 18 below.

In the alternative, refer to the Happinometry table that you have completed for yourself. Choose the elements of misery for which you have given yourself the highest grade. List these elements in the left-hand column of Table 6. Then search through the list of human values on page 124 and evaluate which of them, upon cultivation, will have the greatest impact towards eradicating your particular elements of misery. List these qualities across the top of Table 6. Now complete the rest of the steps outlined in

Table 6
Effect of Human Values in Eradicating the Elements of Misery

Determine several misery elements that you would like to eradicate. List them in the first column. Then select those human qualities that you believe, if cultivated, can eliminate these miseries. Select a number between 1 and 10 for each box that best determines the effect of the human value (listed across the top) on the misery element listed on the left. Leave the box blank if you see no effect between a particular human value and one or more misery elements.

HUMAN VALUES / MISERY ELEMENTS									
TOTAL EFFECT:									

(Add all numbers in each column and write the result above.)

Exercise 18 to assess the hoped-for effect of the human values in reducing the misery elements from which you are suffering.

Exercise 18. *Refer to Table 6 and select up to twenty misery elements that you feel you need to reduce or eliminate. List these elements in the first column (similar to those shown in Table 5). Then select ten qualities from the list of human values on page 124 which you believe can best eliminate or reduce the misery elements that you have selected. List these across the top of Table 6. Now, assess the potential of each human quality in eliminating or reducing each misery element. For example, if you have Love in your list of human values and Arrogance in your list of misery elements, contemplate the possible effect that fostering Love has on reducing Arrogance. Choose a number between 1 and 10, with 10 representing the highest effect and 1 the lowest, and write it in the box across from "Arrogance" and under "Love." Continue in a similar way for all the negative elements in your list, choosing a number between 1 and 10 for each effect, writing it in the appropriate box. Then move to another positive human-quality column and repeat the steps, assessing its possible effect on all the misery elements. If you see no relevance between the positive quality and the misery element considered, leave the box blank. Add all the numbers in each column and enter the totals in the boxes provided. Each of these totals quantifies, for you, the total effect that one human value can have in eliminating or reducing all the misery elements you have selected. Now you have a basis for an action plan. Which human value is most potent in your chart? You may wish to cultivate that human value, which, by quantifying your own beliefs, you have determined has the highest impact on the eradication of your personal elements of misery. On the other hand, you could elect to cultivate the quality which you feel has the highest potential impact on the specific misery element that you suffer from most. The strategy is yours to decide.*

Now that you have identified the human values that you would like to work on, you need a method to cultivate them. The most effective way is to become involved in selfless and unconditional service. The following practices will also help to cultivate human values.

Linkage with a Master as an Effective Way to Cultivate Human Values

A number of relaxation-visualization-meditation methods have been written about, taught, and practiced throughout the country. I have read a few books and taken several seminars that present such techniques. I found most of them to be helpful. In the following, I would like to share a version of a relaxation, visualization, and meditation method that I have practiced myself. It has helped me; I hope it will help you as well.

The method presented here is not in any way meant to replace your own method of mental relaxation, visualization, or meditation, if you already follow and practice one. I urge you to continue that. I invite you to try the method I am suggesting and, if you like it, see if you can incorporate it into your own method.

If you are not following any particular method, I urge you to learn and practice one. A great number of benefits can be drawn from such a practice and the hours required to develop the habit are a worthwhile investment. You can consider the following method as a supplement to such exercises. Presented below is a brief description of what I believe to be a powerful way of cultivating human values.

(a) **Need to identify a Master.** In Chapter 8, I expressed the belief that when the thought of a person occupies our mind, we naturally and gradually develop some of that person's qualities and attributes. Because of this belief, and because Love (translated into unconditional and selfless Service) is the single most important human value for securing happiness, I suggested that you identify several people who symbolize love and unconditional service to you. I referred to these people as Master Teachers or just Masters. The examples I gave for these loving Masters were Moses, Jesus, Mohammed, Zoroaster, Krishna, Buddha, Mary, Mahatma Gandhi, Yogananda, Sai Baba, Mother Theresa, and many others (whom I did not name, but am sure you can identify). If you are not a particularly religious person, or are unfamiliar with these Masters, do yourself the inspiring favor of becoming acquainted intimately with one or more of their lives and teachings. It is important that we keep the thoughts of at least one such Master in mind at all times.

If you haven't done so already, I suggest that you now identify a Master who symbolizes love and compassion to you and has done, or is giving, selfless service. He or She is a person whom you love or can imagine loving and to whom you can easily relate. (In the following discussion, I will be using the pronoun "He" or "Him" to refer to your Master. If your Master is female, please make the appropriate corrections as you read the rest of the text.)

(b) **Common qualities of the Masters.** The Masters I have named above have all the human qualities listed on page 124, and none of the elements of misery. So, if you can keep the thought of your chosen Masters in mind, you are bound to gradually develop and cultivate all of the human values or qualities, and slowly eliminate all those elements of misery. I am absolutely sure about this. With the suggestions made here for relaxation, visualization, and meditation, you can speed up the process of cultivating Human Values.

(c) **Welcoming the Master into your home.** Obtain several pictures of this beloved person and place them in your room, or wherever you can see them often, to be reminded of Him. If you can identify more than one Master, so much the better. Obtain, if you can, the pictures of all these

Masters and, if possible, decorate your residence and office with them.

(d) **Creating your own "Prashanti" corner.** Now, if you can, and if it does not infringe upon the comfort and well-being of the other members of your family, set aside a quiet corner or place in your residence as your own special place. It is here that you will meet your Master(s) during special occasions and during times of meditation and visualization. Give this place a special name, something that identifies peace, joy, serenity, and happiness. Let me borrow a Sanskrit word and call it a "Prashanti" corner, or a place of "ultimate and ever-lasting peace." Decorate your Prashanti corner with your Master's pictures and any other pictures that call forth serenity and peace for you. These could be pictures of roses or other flowers, birds, butterflies, or other animals, or any peaceful and calm scene. Place these pictures, particularly those of your Master(s), at a level where you can see them without bending your neck when you sit down. If you like, select several recordings of soft and relaxing music and some incense of your choice. If you like, obtain some candles, but make sure that there will be no fire hazard when you light them.

(e) **Preparing to pay a special visit to your Master.** Select a time of day that is especially quiet. This can be early morning (usually the best), or late at night. Obtain fresh flowers (particularly roses), if you can, and place them in a suitable location in your Prashanti corner. Make sure you have washed and are perfectly clean and have on clean clothes. Go to your Prashanti corner, start your soft and peaceful music, and light the incense and candle, making sure that there are no fire hazards. Sit in a chair or on the floor, whichever is most comfortable. If you can, obtain a woolen cloth or rug so that you can sit on it, or at least have your feet on it when you sit in a chair. If you sit in a chair, place your feet flat on the floor, easily hold your back and neck straight, and rest your hands on your lap, palms up. If you sit on the floor, make sure your back and neck are straight by sitting cross-legged, and again rest your hands on your lap, palms facing up.

(f) **Expressing thanks and gratitude to the Universe.** While everything is ready and quiet and you are sitting comfortably in your chair or on the floor, close your eyes and mentally thank the Universe for the opportunity that you have to be where you are at this very special time, and for all that you have in your life. Enumerate some of these things: your health, the people in your life, and so on, and the opportunity you have right now for visiting with your Master. Indicate that you are interested in linking with this Master, to possibly see or feel Him in some way, for the express purpose of cultivating human values in yourself. Mentally (or aloud) state that your purpose for all of these activities is to begin fostering love and rendering unconditional and selfless service to all those who may need it. State that you are not seeking any fame or glory with such a possible visit—only to cultivate human values in order to serve better.

(g) **Starting your visualization and meditation.** While your eyes are closed, take several deep breaths through your nose, allowing equal time between the inhalation, holding of the breath, and the exhalation. Make each breath as deep as possible, without straining yourself and without any feelings of discomfort. You can take any number of deep breaths, for example, nine or twelve. While breathing, pay every possible attention to your breath, mentally "riding" along with the molecules of oxygen as they flow into your lungs, "staying" in the lungs, "witnessing" the exchange of oxygen and carbon dioxide taking place inside your lungs, and then "riding" along with the carbon dioxide out of your lungs through your nostrils. After you finish this conscious breathing, while your eyes are still closed, mentally count one to nine, slowly, feeling more relaxed with each count. Mentally say that with each count you are becoming more relaxed. Finally, at the count of nine (or twelve, or any number you have selected) feel yourself completely relaxed, more relaxed than ever before. Feel how relaxed you are. Mentally affirm to yourself that you are very relaxed, several times.

(h) **Creating your "mental Prashanti" space.** To deepen further your level of relaxation, you now mentally enter a beautiful and serene location. This can be a place you have seen in person or in pictures. It can, for example, be a garden, a mountain, a beach, or any place where you feel peaceful and happy. You can mentally create any peaceful and serene space that you want to. Find a name for this beautiful mental creation of yours. As a parallel to your physical Prashanti corner, let me call it your "mental Prashanti space." Now, while your eyes are still closed, mentally enter this beautiful, serene, and calm Prashanti space. Walk around and enjoy whatever is there. See, smell, and feel all the flowers and all that you can perceive about you. Admire the beauty, magnificence, and splendor of the flowers, trees, birds, and animals that you find in your Prashanti space.

(i) **Visiting your Master.** As you walk along, enjoying the serenity and peacefulness of this mentally-created space, you visualize your Master at a distance. He is sitting on a bench looking towards you, as if waiting for you. You walk towards Him and greet Him. He is so happy to see you, and you are indeed very happy to see Him. You both express your delight in seeing each other. He expresses that He loves you very much just the way you are, and He is particularly delighted that you have chosen to cultivate

Human Values within yourself, and that you are deeply interested in strengthening your love and developing a strong desire to serve others selflessly.

Continue to visit and converse with your Master, enjoying every moment of it, feeling happy and joyous to be where you are. Feel how relaxed you can be with this Master, and how happy He is with you. He is a true manifestation of Universal Love and Compassion; love emanates from His eyes and His entire body. You absorb all the love energy that you can from your Master, and enjoy every moment of being where you are.

(j) **Cultivating a specific human value in the presence of your Master.** If you have decided which one of the human values you would like to work on and cultivate, you can bring it up now with your Master. (Let us assume that you want to cultivate Trust in yourself in order to eliminate the misery element of Worry, to be more accepting of other people and of the situations in which you find yourself.) While you are still sitting on the bench, see your Master get up and stand in front of you, holding his hands over and slightly above your head. Now, mentally count from one to three. With the count of three, visualize a bright blue light being emitted by His hands, an intensely beautiful light that covers your entire body. Feel yourself completely immersed in this relaxing, soothing, soft, blue light and mentally affirm:

"I trust the beautiful, magnificent, and abundant Universe to meet all my needs, providing for me, through my own effort, all that I need to have to live comfortably and modestly. I accept and love . . . (name any person or situation) as he, she, or it is, believing that the same loving and generous Universe takes care of them, and provides for them too."

Repeat this affirmation several times. Feel the love that you are receiving from your Master and enjoy feeling completely immersed in the blue light that is charging you with the Human Value, Trust, which you have selected to cultivate.

It is important that you do not let any negative word or statement pass through your mind. In another words, please avoid saying, for example, "I am not worried." Instead, use words such as, "I love and trust the Universe to take care of my needs; I am content and happy about the way things are unfolding for me; all is well in my life." Or, if you are working on the issue of Guilt, instead of saying, "I don't feel guilty," say, "I love myself the way I am; I am a unique and a beautiful human being who possesses all the means of becoming happy and joyous. Indeed, I am a happy and content person."

Mentally repeat these affirmations with your Master as many times as you want, enjoying every moment of being with Him and being immersed in the blue light emitted by Him. He is very interested in knowing that you are making every effort to cultivate human values, and in hearing you speak such affirmations.

(k) **Taking leave of your Master.** When you feel it is time for you to return to your physical Prashanti corner, thank your Master for the opportunity to meet together, and for His spending this time with you. Ask His permission to leave. When He approves your return, bid farewell to Him, and leave your garden or place where you met Him. Now, mentally start counting from one to nine again, saying that with each count your awareness is becoming directed more and more to your physical Prashanti corner. When you reach nine, mentally say, "Now I am fully aware of this location, feeling well and very happy." Repeat the sentence, "I am feeling well and am very happy," several times, and then open your eyes. Feel the peace and serenity that you have experienced and are still enjoying.

Note 1. If you have not had any experience in visualization and meditation before, and even if you have already had such experiences but are more like me, most probably you will have difficulty in quieting your mind and preventing it from jumping around all over the place. Don't give up. We all have this problem. Any time your mind drifts away, try to bring it back, without blaming yourself, or feeling guilty for not being able to concentrate or focus.

If this is the first time you are going to have such an experience, I suggest you go slowly. First, if possible, make the preparations mentioned in steps (a), (c), and (d) above. Then practice steps (e) through (g) for one week, ending by mentally counting from one to nine again, repeating with each count that your awareness is now becoming directed more and more to your Prashanti corner. When you reach nine, mentally say, "Now I am fully aware of this location, feeling well and very happy." Repeat the sentence, "I am feeling well and am very happy," several times and then open your eyes. Feel the peace and serenity that you have experienced and are still enjoying.

After this week, add steps (e) through (h), ending in the same manner discussed above. Do this practice for one week. Then you are ready to follow the entire procedure, using all steps (e) through (k).

Note 2. If you have difficulty visualizing your Master, or seeing yourself immersed in a bubble of blue light, as people often do, still be content that you have been able to relax yourself, and make the affirmations about cultivating Human Values.

Table 7
Timetable for Cultivating Human Values

Select the human values that you would like to cultivate, beginning next month. List (from Table 6) all the misery elements that you feel this particular human value can eradicate.

PERIOD	HUMAN VALUE	THE MISERY ELEMENTS TO BE ERADICATED

Preparing a Timetable for Cultivating Human Values

Cultivation of human values takes times, and we need to be very patient. Table 7 is a timetable that you may want to use in planning to cultivate one Human Value during each month.

In Table 6 (page 130), you determined the effects or impacts of each Human Value on the eradication or reduction of misery elements. Now, select from this table those human values that you want to cultivate most in order to eliminate the related miseries. Select the period that you would like to work, indicating the day and the month. Complete this table for at least five human values.

To have more fun cultivating each human value you select, gather pictures, make drawings and posters, or create things that symbolize those qualities. Place these all around your house or place of residence. For example, if you have chosen to cultivate contentment as a human value during the month of May, then make or gather posters, cards, pictures, quotations, cartoons, and so on, that remind you to be content with all you have. Let the whole world know that the month of May is "contentment month" for you.

If you choose the month of November to be your thanksgiving and gratitude month, in addition to all the above visual affirmations, make every effort to express your gratitude first to your family, then to all people, society, and your country for whatever they have done for you (no matter how small it may seem to you). Of course, express your greatest thanks to the Universe.

Exercise 19. *Complete Table 7 for five human values that you would like to cultivate during the next five months, beginning the first day of next month. Complete the preparatory steps, (a), (c), and (d) mentioned above under "Linking with a Master to Cultivate Human Values," before the month begins.*

Starting the first day of the month, consider the human quality that you have selected to work on in Table 7. Follow steps (e) through (k) mentioned in the above section. Do this exercise as often as you can, preferably twice daily, early in the morning and late at night. During all other times, keep the thoughts of your Master in mind constantly, concentrating on the strength of that human value in Him. Read as much as you can on the cultivation of this value and about the people who truly possess this human quality.

Complete a Happinometry table at the end of this month and compare it with that of the previous month. Is there a difference in your happiness value?

Group Visualization/Meditation for Cultivating Human Values

The visualization/meditation method and the linkage with a Master that I described above can also be used in a group. A group effort is almost always more effective than an individual one. To carry out this activity in a group, I recommend the following:

1. If you have friends who have the same belief as you do, who strongly desire to cultivate human values, and who have familiarity with meditation or visualization practice, or who have been following the method suggested in this chapter, try to get together with them and form a Human-Values Cultivation group. In your first meeting, find yourself a good name, and go by it, a name which brings to mind the human values, and the need for cultivating these values and qualities.

2. Find a suitable time of the week and a cozy, quiet place for your weekly gathering. If most nights of the week are all right, how about considering Thursday night? I know there are many similar meditation activities normally held on this night. By scheduling your activity on Thursday nights, you may be able to receive the greater benefit of a larger group cultivating human values throughout the world.

   Your place of gathering might be in somebody's home, in a school, or in any other convenient place. If you can, decorate this place permanently with peaceful, serene, and relaxing pictures, and with the pictures of the Masters of the participants. If a permanent decoration is not possible, then ask everyone to bring one or more pictures of his or her Master for each meeting, and decorate the place temporarily for the purpose.

3. If none of the group is sensitive to candles or incense, and if there is no fire hazard, select these, and possibly some soft, relaxing music with which everyone is comfortable. Remember that candles, music, and incense are not absolutely essential, but can sometimes help the relaxation process.

4. Consider a timetable such as Table 7 for the group, deciding a common human value for the whole group to cultivate during each month. Try to work out a calendar for the year or for the next six months. It is very helpful if everyone in the group concentrates on one human quality during the entire month.

5. Find one member of the group who has a relaxing voice to lead the group for visualization/meditation and linkage with the Masters. This person can later record his or her words, so that he or she can join the process too.

6. With everyone sitting comfortably in one's place, being able to easily see the picture of his or her Master, and with

the candles and incense lit and the soft music playing, begin the linkage process. Here is what your visualization/meditation guide would say very quietly and very softly to help the group activity:

(a) "Please look at the picture of your Master and keep that picture in mind. Now close your eyes and be very relaxed and comfortable." While everyone's eyes are closed, continue, "We are grateful to the Universe for the opportunity we now have to gather here to cultivate love and other human values in ourselves. We are also thankful to our Masters who have accepted our invitations to be with us during this period. Our intention in this gathering and in this exercise is to foster and cultivate human values in order to be happier and love and serve others unconditionally and more effectively."

(b) "Please take a deep breath." (You need to consider the depth of the breath that everyone is comfortable with and no one is strained by. It is necessary to find this out ahead of time.) "Pay attention to your breath, riding along with the air going into your lungs. Hold your breath, paying attention to the exchange of oxygen and carbon dioxide in your lungs. Exhale, riding along with the carbon dioxide leaving your lungs through your nostrils." Repeat this procedure any number of times (between 5 and 12) that is comfortable for the group.

(c) "Now I will count from one to nine, and with each count you feel more relaxed. One . . . two . . . three. (Count very slowly.) You are now becoming more relaxed. Four . . . five . . . six. You are getting into a very deep state of relaxation. Seven . . . eight. . . . You are now more relaxed than ever before. Feel how relaxed you are, you are very, very relaxed, calm and peaceful. With the count of nine you will reach the deepest level of relaxation. Nine. You are very relaxed and calm. Feel how relaxed and serene you are."

(d) "To reach an even more complete state of relaxation, now enter your mental Prashanti space." (Everyone who has been practicing the exercise suggested earlier in this chapter should have such a space.) "See how beautiful this place is—very beautiful, relaxing, calm, and serene. You feel very relaxed and happy to be here.

"As you walk and enjoy the serenity and the peacefulness of this place, you see your Master sitting on a bench at a far distance. Walk towards Him. Greet Him, and mentally tell Him how happy you are to see Him and be with Him. He invites you to sit next to Him. He then tells you that He is so very happy to see you, that He loves you very much and is happy that you have begun cultivating love and other human values. He assures you that He will support you all the way and will assist you in your efforts. He tells you that you can call on Him any time you want. He tells you that He is always available and never farther away than your own heart.

"You mentally tell Him that you and your friends are all gathered here to cultivate . . . (name the human value of the month). You ask Him to assist you. He agrees. He then gets up and stands in front of you, holding His hands over you, a short distance away from your head. You mentally count from one to three and, with the count of three, you see that a bright blue light is being emitted by His hands. The light covers your entire body. Feel yourself completely immersed in this bubble of soft, beautiful and peaceful light. Feel that this blue light is charging you with love, with the desire to serve selflessly, and it strengthens you in . . . (name the human value selected for the month and restructure the sentence if necessary. Make sure you are not using any negative term or inducing any negativity. See the discussion of step (j) in the previous section. Make a proper sentence, suitable for the human value selected, for everyone to affirm mentally. Ask everyone to repeat that affirmation several times.)

(e) "Feel how well this human value and quality is being cultivated in you. Feel how happy and relaxed you are to have this important human quality. (Repeat this last sentence several times.)

(f) "Now it is time to bid farewell to your Master and return your attention to this place. I will now count from one to nine, and with each count your attention and awareness will become directed more and more completely to this present time and place. One . . . two . . . three. Your attention is now being directed to this room. Four . . . five . . . six. You have left your mental Prashanti and are returning to this place, feeling very well and happy, remembering everything that you have witnessed. Seven . . . eight. . . . With the count of nine, I would like you to open your eyes, feeling completely relaxed and happy, feeling completely well and joyous. Nine. Open your eyes, feeling very relaxed, serene, and very, very happy."

7. Remain quiet for a few moments to allow all participants to open their eyes. Stop the music, then ask if anyone would like to share his or her experience, and if anyone has any comment on the conduct of the relaxation, visualization, meditation, and linkage with his or her Master.

The Role of Government in Cultivating Human Values

State and Federal governments, with their financial and human resources, can play important roles in cultivating the human values discussed in this chapter. Their most important role can be to:

Establish Centers or Institutes for Research Into Cultivation
of Human Values, (Centers for RICH-Values.)

Without going into any detailed discussions, some highlights
of other efforts that can be undertaken by governments include:

1. Providing every means possible for parents (preferably
   mothers) of preschool and grade school children to be at
   home whenever the children are, to spend more time with
   them, to nurture them, and to give them love and teach
   them human values.

2. Subsidizing the media to promote, in their programs, love,
   respect, reverence, and appreciation of nature; showing
   the lifestyles of those who have served, or are serving,
   unconditionally, and selflessly.

3. Subsidizing the media to produce programs that foster and
   cultivate other human values.

4. Subsidizing the media not to show or cover violence in
   their programming.

5. Subsidizing the media not to pay so much attention to the
   physical aspects of human life; particularly de-emphasizing
   extravagant living.

6. Subsidizing or encouraging the media to foster modest
   living, conservation of natural resources, and placing a
   ceiling on desires.

7. Initiating programs that eradicate the indignity of joblessness.

8. Initiating comprehensive health care plans to reduce or
   remove worries over the high cost of hospitalization and
   health care.

11

HAPPINESS IS THE BEST MEDICINE

We can only be as healthy as we think it is possible to be.
Nature is giving us only the reality we expect and believe in.

—Deepak Chopra

Our body's immune system fights diseases more effectively
when we are happy rather than depressed.

—David Myers

The relationship between body, mind, and spirit is an ancient wisdom and is well accepted by psychologists. Many incidents show how the power of one's mind and belief system can affect one's health and well-being.

The Power of Mind and Belief to Affect One's Health— a Few Examples

In Chapter 5, I shared with you my meeting with a medical doctor who practiced medicine in three different places. He used to prescribe the same medicine for the same symptoms, but the healing rate was not the same in all those places; it was the highest where the patients had the greatest faith in him and his medicine, and the lowest where exactly the opposite was true. I would like to share the following stories with you which further show how the power of mind can bring on illness and even death, and how it can also heal a completely paralyzed person.

Office employees help to bring illness to a colleague. In a government office, where the employees spent more time talking and sharing with each other about their personal lives than working, a mischievous man, who had read about the power of mind and belief, decided to run an experiment. He targeted Jeff, a conscientious employee of whom he was jealous, as his research object. He talked to his colleagues about the experiment he was going to carry out, and invited them to participate and cooperate. They all agreed, because they did not have much work to do and were interested in learning about the outcome.

Starting the next day, anyone who saw Jeff asked him if he felt all right. Jeff would say, "Of course, why did you ask?"

The person would reply, "Oh, nothing, I just wanted to know, because you look pale and tired."

Jeff would reply, "No, I am fine." The next person who met Jeff would ask him the same question, and Jeff would answer the same. These people approached Jeff in a very normal and casual manner, so there was no doubt in Jeff's mind that they were seeing in him what he couldn't see himself. After several people asked Jeff the same question and made the same comments, he started wondering about his condition. During the lunch break, a woman employee who knew Jeff's wife called her to say hello and asked her if there was anything wrong with Jeff. She elaborated that she thought Jeff was not feeling well in the office.

By late afternoon, Jeff started developing the symptoms that his colleagues were describing; he became pale and started feeling tired and sick. When he got home, his wife greeted him in the normal fashion, but saw that Jeff was really feeling sick. She commented on his condition and thought he should see his doctor the next day. Jeff called his boss the next day to report his sickness.

Jeff was absent from the office for a couple of days before his colleagues decided to reveal their terrible research plan to him. They all decided to go and see him at his house. They revealed that what they had done was just an experiment and there was indeed nothing wrong with him. They revealed that *he became sick because of his belief that he was sick*.

Jeff was back at his office the next day.

A refrigeration engineer wills himself to death. An engineer who was inspecting the refrigeration system of a freight car on a late Friday afternoon was accidentally locked inside by another employee who was closing the place for the weekend. His banging on the doors and walls of the car and yelling for help to let him out were not heard by anyone, and he was trapped inside for the entire weekend. The freight car was empty, but was designed to carry frozen foods.

The engineer became very frightened over his predicament. He knew that the human body cannot endure sub-freezing temperatures for long—definitely not as long as the weekend. He knew that there was a sufficient amount of air for him, and that he could survive with no water or food for that period of confinement. What bothered him was that his body definitely could not endure the low temperature of the freight car. He knew that he would definitely die by Monday morning.

With his mind set about his predicament, he decided to help science and let the others know what he was going through, by describing the ordeal of freezing to death. He decided to write his condition on the wall of the car every 15 minutes.

At 5:15, he wrote about his condition, how he was trapped inside the car, and how he intended to spend his last few hours helping humankind learn about the feelings of a man freezing to death. At 5:30, he wrote that he had started feeling cold in his extremities, at 5:45, that he was already feeling cold in his arms and legs. He continued writing his feelings every 15 minutes. At 11:00, he wrote that his body was nearly frozen, that he could hardly hold his pen, and that he would not be around for long. At 11:30 pm, he wrote that this must be his last message, as he was completely freezing, despite the fact that he was trying to keep his hand warm enough to write further. Sure enough, that was the last message he wrote.

When the employees opened the door of this freight car on Monday morning, they found the body of their colleague on the floor. They immediately informed the police that he was found and to stop searching for him elsewhere. They also saw all the notes he had written on the wall of the car. But, to their amazement, they found that the refrigeration system of the car was out of order, and had never operated in the past several days. Through further investigation, it was revealed to them that the temperature never went below the freezing point at all; in fact, it was well above this range. They knew that the human body can easily endure these temperatures, and their friend could not have died due to low temperatures.

The man had simply willed himself to death.

A man wills himself to health.* Morris was involved in a plane crash and injured his spinal cord at several places. He became completely paralyzed; he could see and hear other people and understand his surroundings, but was unable to share his thoughts and feelings with anyone. The doctor who examined him suggested that he and his family would have to cope with this situation for the rest of his life. Since there was no way that Morris could communicate with his family or anyone else, the doctor suggested that he blink his eyes once to answer yes, and twice for answering no. Morris was aware of his predicament, but did not believe that he would have to live with his condition for the rest of his life. He utilized the doctor's suggestion and kept blinking his eyes repeatedly. The doctor, the nurses, and his family, who

---

*   I am sharing this story from a video I saw several years ago. It was called "The Miracle Man." There is a book by the same title, but I have not read it.

were all at his bedside, realized that he wanted to say something. So they got him an alphabet board and started pointing to various letters. He chose the letters he wanted by blinking his eyes once and rejected the rest by blinking twice. After a long trial, he finally made a sentence.

Morris's sentence was to the effect that on such and such a date (exactly one year from the date of the accident), he was going to walk out of the hospital on his own feet. The doctor, who had already spent his time waiting for him to make a sentence, became annoyed and angry that this patient was already defying him. He told Morris that the fact that he was alive and able to see and hear was a miracle. He told Morris and his family that they should be happy and grateful for his being alive and should try to accept his condition and make the best of it. Morris made another sentence to the effect that six months after the first accomplishment (again giving the exact date), he was going to walk into the doctor's office and thank him for his treatment. His third and last sentence was, "Doctor, I think you are great."

Morris had heard about the fate of the refrigeration engineer (the story I shared with you above) when he was young. He argued with himself, and came to believe that if a man's mind is powerful enough to will himself to death, it should also be powerful enough to will himself to health. So, he decided to go against all the odds and predictions of modern medicine. He believed that he could heal himself, and he was determined to accomplish it.

Morris was the president of a manufacturing firm and was familiar with short-range and long-range planning. In fact, he always did that in his work. Here, for his healing process, his long-range goal and plan was to walk out of the hospital on his own feet in a year's time. His short range plans were to accomplish specific tasks, one at a time, during a specified time. In addition to setting his mind to and concentrating on accomplishing what he had planned, he really worked hard to achieve what he wanted. For example, he worked really hard just to learn to drink water.

He did the same for all the skills he needed to master in order to get back on his feet and walk.

On exactly the date that Morris had predicted one year earlier, he was wheeled to the hospital door by a nurse. He asked the nurse to keep the door open for him. He got up from his wheelchair and, taking one short step at a time, very carefully and watching not to lose his balance, he walked out of the hospital on his own feet. He went home for further therapy. Six months later, he returned to the doctor's office driving his own car, to thank him for treating him and being patient with him all this time.

The doctor commented, "You are indeed the miracle man that all the patients and nurses in the hospital have come to call you. You went against all the odds and *willed yourself back to health.*"

Recent Research into Mind/Body Connectedness

The examples I shared above are but three cases that show how truly powerful our minds are. I am sure you have heard similar stories about how the belief of a patient worked for or against him or her. However, the relation between mind and body is only now being rediscovered by modern biology and medicine. The interest in this relationship is evidenced by the number of books written by medical doctors in the past few years. I have given the names of the authors and the titles of some of these books in the bibliography (4, 10-14.) Here are a few excerpts.

Deliman and Smolowe discuss the concept of holism in their book, *Holistic Medicine: Harmony of Body, Mind and Spirit,* and state that, "Most central to holistic philosophy are the ideas of wholeness or oneness of entities and the existence of functional interdependence among parts and wholes."(10)

In their book, *The Healer Within: The New Medicine of Mind and Body,* Locke and Colligan state, "Among the goals of psychoneuroimmunology is finding the way to summon hope. Part of its quest is to call forth the *biology of hope* through an appreciation of the healing powers of the human spirit and a deeper under-standing of the intimate neuronal and hormonal bonds between the mind and the body."(11)

Deepak Chopra, in discussing the body/mind relationship in his book, *Perfect Health*, states, "No one has proved that getting sick is necessary. Quite the opposite. We choose our own diseases, but we are not aware of this choice, because it takes place at a level below our everyday thoughts. The ideal of perfect health depends upon perfect balance. Everything we eat, say, think, do, see, and feel affects our overall state of balance."(13)

Elliot Dacher, in his book, *Psychoneuroimmunology (PNI): The New Mind/Body Healing Program*, reviews the current research in the relationship between mind, body, and spirit, and draws the following conclusions:(14)

"Holistic healers focus on the individual, not the disease. They enlist the individual as a partner in a healing program which encompasses mind, body, and spirit." Under the heading of mind/body conversations, Dr. Dacher states:

"The brain appears to play the central administrative role in translating the content of the mind, attitude, and perceptions into nerve impulses and biochemistry. It then communicates with the body through the nervous system, consisting of nerves extending from the brain to the remainder of the body and biochemicals that circulate throughout the body."

He continues:

"The central nervous system (CNS) is an important link be-tween mind and body. It translates the intention to move a muscle into the electrical nerve impulses that result in movement of our arms and legs.

"The neuropeptide chemical messenger system is the most re-cently discovered system that connects mind with the body. The neuropeptides are produced both by brain cells and by cells through-out the body, including the hormonal and immune cells. Not only is the brain, through the neuropeptides, able to communicate directly with the body, activating the immune and hormonal systems, but the body, by producing these same chemicals, is able to communicate back to the brain, activating the brain cells. . . . What is unfolding is an extraordinary intercommunication system between brain and body that compels us to now view the brain and body as a dynamic interactive network.

"The final, and most exciting piece of information, is that *the production of these chemicals in the brain can be turned on and off by certain mental states.* . . . This final link confirms the age-old wisdom that mind and body are intimately connected and interactive. Our emotions, perceptions, and attitudes exist not only in our mind but also are reflected in the physiology of our body." Dr. Dacher continues:

"We are now confirming the capacity of *the individual through his or her attitudes and actions, to self-regulate the most minute aspects of the biochemistry and physiology of the mind and body.* Applied to the immune system, this means that an individual can choose to either enhance or suppress it and similarly affect the function of other important physiologic systems of the body.

"Beyond these implications is the important recognition that other individuals, to the extent that their attitudes and actions have a direct influence on our mental state, can also influence and control our physiology. When we become angry, stressed, feel victimized, experience joy or any other strong emotion as a direct result of our interaction with others, our physiology responds to these emotions and is thereby connected to and controlled by the attitudes and actions of the other individual. It is possible for anyone to influence directly the most minute biochemical reactions in another individual's body. This may give credence to the comment, 'You make me sick,' and the observation that some individuals appear to be very powerful healers. The yogis, who were well aware of the vulnerability of an untrained and unsteady mind, cautioned their students to maintain a benign indifference towards those who would cause them distress and goodwill towards those who are content.

"Consider further how the mental state of a powerful leader, or the imperatives of a strongly held cultural value or belief can influence the mental state and physiology of an entire group of individuals. Followed to its end, the research in PNI may well validate and amplify the discoveries of quantum physics and the metaphysical insights of the yogis; *all is connected, all is interactive, all is one.* It may, in fact, be true that none of us can be completely healed until we are all healed."

On the question of genetically-caused diseases, Dr. Dacher states that, "Although the genetic factors are not under our control, the degree to which the genetic tendency becomes manifest as actual disease can be significantly affected by mind-style and life-style."(14)

This oneness and connectedness that Dr. Dacher concludes directly confirms the interdependence of our happiness with the happiness and well-being of other beings. It means that to maximize our own happiness we must pay attention to the happiness of other people. Of course, bringing joy to other people is a service which will directly bring us joy and happiness.

Let me continue with other research in the area of mind/body connectedness. Louise Hay, in her book, *Heal Your Body,*(2) discusses the mental causes for physical illness and suggests metaphysical ways to overcome them. She believes that for every disease there is a mental pattern responsible for it; it can be healed if the pattern causing the disease is reversed. She gives her own example, of how she was able to heal herself of cancer. She realized that she needed to clear her old pattern of resentment by doing a great deal of forgiving. Along with the mental cleansing and good nutrition to detoxify her body, she was able to heal her cancer in six months. She states,(2)

> "I know that if the clients are willing to do the mental work of releasing and forgiving, almost anything can be healed. The word 'incurable,' which is so frightening to so many people, really only means that the particular condition cannot be cured by outer methods and that we must go within to effect the healing."

Dr. Hay further explains, "If we want a joyous life, we must think joyous thoughts. Whatever we send out mentally or verbally will come back to us in like form. . . . Be willing to change your words and thoughts and watch your life change. The way to control your life is to control your choice of words and thoughts."(2)

Dr. Hay has worked out a table which relates various diseases to their mental causes. She has found that the mental thought patterns that cause most diseases are criticism, anger, guilt, and resentment.(2) Going through this table, we notice that almost all the causes of diseases that she lists are the ones we have referred to as the elements of misery in Chapter 3.

This is a very important relationship. It shows that happiness and health are very strongly related to one another. That is, if I want to be happier, I need to reduce or eliminate the elements of misery from which I am suffering, and about which we have been discussing in this book. On the other hand, if I want to be healthier, I also need to eliminate the same miseries from my life. Referring to the Happinometry equation,

$(H = J - F - E)$, we see that by reducing these misery elements, we can reduce both F and E, contributing doubly to increase H. In short, *if I want to be healthy, I need to be happy.*

The Role of Diet in Securing Health

In addition to the thoughts we think and the beliefs we hold, the food we eat and the liquid we drink have a direct influence on our physical well-being and health. It is therefore important that we pay attention to the food we eat and plan a healthy and nutritious diet.

David Reuben, in his book, *The Save-Your-Life Diet,* considers the diet of industrialized societies to be short of fiber, and this alone to be the cause of several life-threatening illnesses. He adds, "There seems little doubt that adding the missing roughage to our diet provides protection from: cancer of the colon and rectum, ischemic heart disease—the prime cause of heart attacks, diverticular disease of the colon, appendicitis, phlebitis and the resulting blood clots to the lungs, and obesity."(15) To convert to a high-roughage diet, Dr. Reuben suggests:

1. Use only whole-grain products such as whole wheat, brown rice, and so on.

2. Consume fresh fruits and vegetables raw or barely cooked with seeds, strings, and skins intact, if at all possible.

3. Cut to a bare minimum consumption of refined sugar, soft drinks, fats, and meat.(15)

Dr. Dacher, in his book referred to above, suggests the following diets for the circulatory system:(14)

1. Reduce the intake of salt.

2. Reduce the intake of animal products (meat, dairy, and eggs), which provide cholesterol and saturated fats.

3. Do not smoke.

For the gastrointestinal system he suggests:

1. Emphasize carbohydrate, fiber, and unprocessed foods, which are foods that have taken a minimal detour from the farm to your grocery store.

2. Minimize animals fats.

3. Drink lots of water.

4. Have modest-sized meals that you chew and eat slowly with mindfulness.

For the immune system, Dr. Dacher writes that, "The small amount of available information suggests that elevated fats and obesity (or either condition separately) act to suppress the immune system, and yellow and orange vegetables serve to enhance the immune system."(14)

Andrew Weil, in his book, *Natural Health, Natural Medicine*, gives rather comprehensive information on how to prevent and treat illnesses and in general how to maintain optimal health.(16)

Depending on the type of work we do, we need to find out the best diet and exercise for us. It is delightful to see so many people developing exercise plans and, through these and a careful diet, making every effort to maintain good health. I have seen many people doing away with meats and becoming vegetarians. Millions of people in Asia and other parts of the world are strict vegetarians and enjoy good health. I know several families who gave up eating meat a long time ago, and who don't miss it a bit. They tell me that they are healthier and happier.

I met a young family several years ago who were on a strict vegetarian diet. When I asked them how long they had been abstaining from meat, Mrs. S.W. said, "It is about 16 years that we have not had any meat." She continued that when she was pregnant with her first son about 14 years ago, she received a lot of advice and comments from people who were concerned about the health of her fetus. Among them was her own medical-doctor brother, who called her long distance to advise her on the importance of her consuming meat for the sake of her baby. She said she consulted her husband about the issue of remaining vegetarian during her pregnancy and found him to be very supportive of her decision. She decided to remain a vegetarian. Mrs. S.W. never regrets her decision. Now she has two athletically active boys who have never had any meat in their lives.

In addition to better health, reducing meat consumption or becoming vegetarian has several important environmental benefits. Among many advantages, one is that the land currently under cultivation to grow feedstock could be converted to forests or national parks. Another advantage is the reduction of widespread underground water pollution, which has its source in the runoff from cattle ranches and stockyards, plus a reduction in methane gas, which is a cause of global warming trend.

The above discussion can be summarized as follows:

By developing a proper attitude and belief system and by adapting proper diet and physical exercise, we can secure a healthy and happy life. Then, we can enjoy long life, without any of the symptoms or appearances generally associated with old age.

The following story shows all of these are possible.

The Young-Looking Old People

A retired British Army officer who had heard about a special monastery in Northern India, decided to go and live there for a few years. The unique aspect of this monastery was, as he had heard, that everyone who lived there looked twenty to thirty years younger than his or her age.

When the officer left for his adventure, he was 67, with grey hair. He was balding, wearing glasses, frail, and very weak. When he returned after living there for about two years, he did not have any of the symptoms associated with old age. For example, he did not need any glasses, he had grown full dark hair and was very robust. His features had so drastically changed that his friends had a hard time recognizing him at first. In fact, when a friend of his invited a number of people to hear the story of this officer, he first asked the guests to guess the officer's age and write it down on a piece of paper. The average age guessed by these people was about 45 years old. The officer thanked them laughingly, and told them that he was going to celebrate his 70th birthday the next week. He then went on to share details of his life in the monastery, which helped him to rejuvenate.

Lifestyle in the old-people's monastery. The officer told his audience that the monastery was located in a remote area, far away from any road or major city. When he arrived there and was accepted to join the group, everybody referred to him as "the old man," because he looked older than anybody else in the compound. Later, he learned that most of the people living there were much older than he was.

The officer went on to say that in the monastery everyone worked to take care of the needs of the compound. They grew their own food and were mostly independent of the outside world. He further described the lifestyle in the monastery as follows:

1. A strict vegetarian diet.

2. Chewing of the food for a long time.

3. Strict silence during the meal times. Thoughts were directed in expressing gratitude to the Universe and in helping to assimilate the food.

4. Careful balancing of each meal, by mixing various foods with each other for any meal.

5. Spending a great deal of time in silence, in individual and group meditations.

6. Constant thinking and praying for the welfare of humanity and the environment.

7. Carrying out special group exercises each day.

If a small number of old people can work and live modestly and be healthy and happy, why can't we all do the same?

Linkage with a Master as an Effective Way to Maintain Health and Aid in the Healing Process

In Chapter 10, I presented a relaxation, visualization, and meditation technique, and talked about how to mentally link with your Master to cultivate human values. I would like to suggest the same procedure for health maintenance and for helping any healing process which may be taking place to restore your health.

I should emphasize that the method suggested here is not a substitute for the healing and health maintenance procedures that you are already following. I don't claim that by practicing this method you will be healed of any illness that you may have. I suggest this procedure only as a supplement, and not a substitute, to whatever procedure you are now following in this matter. I have been using the procedure suggested herein myself and enjoy the relaxation resulted by it. I am very grateful to the Universe for the good health that I have enjoyed all my life.

1. If possible, make the preparations outlined in (a), (c), and (d), and take the steps (e) thorough (i) outlined on pages 132-137 in Chapter 10.

2. Visualize your Master standing in front of you, with His hands over and slightly above your head. Mentally count from one to three and, with the count of three, visualize a bright, golden light being emitted by your Master's hands, covering your body completely. You are totally immersed in a bubble of bright golden light. Feel how enjoyable and relaxing it is to be totally submerged in the loving, bright, golden light, with its immense physical healing power. Mentally see the light particularly concentrated in the area of your body where you are feeling pain or which needs healing. See that part of the body as already healed and functioning properly. Concentrate the light on any malignant cells and tissues, if such are present in your body, seeing the light eliminating these cells and tissues while having no effect on the healthy ones. Feel this process for as long as you like, visualizing your Master as standing in front of you, still holding His hands over your head, and still radiating your body with the healing golden light.

   Your Master asks you how you are feeling. You mentally thank Him, say that you are just fine, and affirm that every cell, every tissue, every muscle, every bone, and every organ of your body is in perfect health, functioning perfectly in total harmony with respect to each other and with respect to the Universe, and you are indeed very healthy and very happy. Repeat this affirmation several times in the presence of your Master.

Make sure that you do not allow any negative statements, thoughts, or words to pass through you. For example, please avoid saying that you do not feel any pain in
your knees. Instead, say that your knees are healthy and
functioning properly. See and feel that they are indeed so.

3. Now prepare to return your attention and awareness to
your Prashanti corner by following step (k) described in the
section and chapter mentioned above, or continue on to
the next visualization/meditation exercise.

Linkage with a Master to Help Mental Concentration Power

1. If possible, make the preparations outlined in (a), (c), and
(d), and take steps (e) through (i) outlined on pages
132-137 in Chapter 10.

2. Visualize and feel your Master's presence, standing in front
of you, holding His hands above your head. Count from
one to three and, with the count of three, visualize a bright,
yellow light being emitted by His hands, covering and
going through your entire body. Feel yourself totally immersed in this beautiful, relaxing bubble of bright, yellow
light. Mentally affirm that you have great ability to concentrate your attention and your mind on your job or
anything you desire. Think about one of the problems that
has occupied your mind or for which you are seeking a
solution. See the problem as already solved and you as
relieved by it, very happy with the solution you have found.
Feel the joy of accomplishment in having solved a problem
that has been bothering you for some time. (A solution may
reach your mind right then, when you are relaxed, or it may
come some time in the future. Either way, see the problem
as already solved.)

3. You can now return to your Prashanti corner, following step (k) as outlined on page 138.

Linkage with a Master for Total Benefit

It is possible to combine the above visualizations for healing benefits and for increasing powers of concentration with the one for cultivating positive human values outlined in the previous chapter to draw combined benefit from the experience. I have practiced this myself for the past several years and enjoyed it greatly. I have also conducted the same activity in a weekly group meeting with good results.

I highly recommend this combination to you, if you can spend a little longer time every day in this process. Otherwise, you may wish to continue one of the procedures we have talked about so far, perhaps devoting the weekends, or any time you can afford a longer period of time, to this activity. The following exercise best describes the combined procedure.

Exercise 20. *Consider a human value that you would like to work on and cultivate, a healing process for a particular place in your body, and a problem for which you would like to find a solution.*

1. If possible, make the preparations (a), (c), and (d) outlined on pages 132-137. Then, take steps (e) through (i) of that section.

2. Feel the presence of your Master, standing in front of you, holding His hands over and above your head. Mentally count from one to three and, with the count of three, visualize a bright blue light being emitted by your Master's hands, covering your entire body. Feel yourself totally immersed in a bubble of beautiful, relaxing, bright blue light. Feel and mentally affirm that with this light you are

---

Exercise continues on next page.

now completely charged with love, forgiveness, compassion, desire to render selfless service, and the human value that you have decided to cultivate. Feel yourself charged with such qualities, and repeat the above affirmation several times, while you still feel immersed in the blue light, and while your Master is still standing in front of you with His hands above your head.

3. Still feeling the presence of your Master standing in front of you, with His hands above your head, mentally count from one to three and, on the count of three, visualize a bright golden light being emitted by the Master's hands, covering your entire body. Feel and enjoy being immersed in the bubble of bright golden light. Visualize that this light rejuvenates your entire body, particularly healing the part that needs treatment. Mentally affirm that every cell, every tissue, every muscle, every bone, and every organ of your body is in perfect health and functioning perfectly in total harmony with respect to each other and with respect to the Universe. Affirm that you are perfectly healthy and totally happy. Repeat the last affirmation several times.

4. Next, still feeling your Master's presence as before, mentally count from one to three and, with the count of three, visualize a bright yellow light being emitted by your Master's hands and covering you completely. Feel yourself totally immersed in this beautiful, relaxing bubble of yellow light. Mentally affirm that you have great ability to concentrate your attention and your mind on your job or anything you desire. Think about the problem that has occupied your mind for which you are seeking a solution. See the problem as being already solved, and you being relieved by it, being very happy with the solution. Feel the joy of accomplishment in having solved a problem that has been bothering you for some time. (A solution may reach your mind right then, while being relaxed, or at some time in the future. Either way, see the problem as being already solved.)

5. Stay in the condition you are in as long as you can, enjoying the peace and serenity which the Universe has granted you.

6. You can now return to your Prashanti corner, following step (k) outlined on page 138, Chapter 10.

Group Visualization/Meditation to Aid Health Maintenance and the Healing Process

This is very similar to the group effort in the visualization/meditation, and the linkage-with-a-Master method that I described in the previous chapter for cultivating human values. Here I repeat the activity, and highly recommend that you carry it out for helping your own health maintenance and healing process as well as that of others. Group efforts are always more effective than the individual ones.

1. If you have friends who have the same belief as you do, who strongly desire to maintain their own health and help the healing process through meditation and linkage with a Master, who have been practicing a meditation or visualization technique, or who at least have been following the method suggested in this and the preceding chapters, try to get together with them and form a group.

2. Find a suitable time of the week and a cozy, quiet place for your weekly gathering. This place can be in someone's home, in a school, or in any other convenient place. If you can, decorate this place permanently with peaceful, serene, and relaxing pictures, and with the pictures of the Masters of the participants. If a permanent decoration is not possible, then ask everyone to bring one or more pictures of his or her Master every time you meet, and decorate the place temporarily for the purpose.

3. If none of the group is sensitive to candles or incense, and if there is no fire hazard, select these, plus soft, relaxing music with which everyone is comfortable. Remember that candles, music, and incense are not absolutely essential, but can help the relaxation process greatly.

4. Find one of the members of the group who has a relaxing voice to lead the group for visualization/meditation and

linkage with the Masters. This person can later record his or her words, so that he or she can join the activity too.

5. With everyone seated comfortably in their places, each being able easily to see the picture of his or her Master, with candles and incense lit and soft music playing, begin the linkage process. Here is what your visualization/meditation guide would say, very quietly and very softly, to help the group activity:

(a) "Please sit up straight with your spinal cord and neck in a straight line. Look at the picture of your Master and keep that picture in mind. Now close your eyes and be very relaxed and comfortable." While everyone's eyes are closed, continue, "We are grateful to the Universe for the opportunity we now have to gather here to cultivate love, and to help our health maintenance and healing processes. We are also thankful to our Masters, who have accepted our invitations to be with us during this period. Our intention in this gathering and in this exercise is to maintain our health and heal ourselves in order to be happier, and to love and serve others unconditionally and more effectively."

(b) "Please take a deep breath. (You need to consider the depth of breath with which everyone is comfortable and by which no one is strained. It is necessary to find this out ahead of time.) Pay attention to your breath, riding along with the air going into your lungs. Hold your breath, paying attention to the exchange of oxygen and carbon dioxide in your lungs. Exhale, riding along with the carbon dioxide leaving your lungs through your nostrils. (Repeat this procedure any number of times, between 5 and 12, that is comfortable for the group.)

(c) "Now I will count from one to nine, and with each count you will feel more relaxed. One . . . two . . .

three. . . . (Count very slowly.) You are now becoming more relaxed. Four . . . five . . . six. You are getting into a very deep state of relaxation. Seven . . . eight. . . . You are now more relaxed than ever before. Feel how relaxed you are; you are very, very relaxed, calm and peaceful. With the count of nine you will reach the deepest level of relaxation. Nine. You are very relaxed and calm. Feel how relaxed and serene you are.

(d) "To reach an even more complete state of relaxation, you now enter your mental Prashanti space." (Everyone who has been practicing the exercises suggested earlier in the previous chapter should have such a mentally-created space.) "See how beautiful this place is. It is very beautiful, relaxing, calm, and serene. You feel very relaxed and happy in this place. Walk around, see, smell, feel, and experience the flowers, plants, and everything there is in this beautiful place. You are indeed very relaxed and happy to be here.

(e) "As you walk and enjoy the serenity and the peacefulness of this place, you see your Master sitting on a bench at a far distance. Walk towards Him. Greet Him and mentally tell Him how happy you are to see Him and be with Him. He invites you to sit next to him. He then tells you that He is indeed happy to see you, that He loves you very much and is very happy for you to have started this linkage activity. He tells you that He will support you all the way and will assist you in your efforts. He asks you just to call on Him any time you want. He tells you that He is always available. You mentally tell Him that you and your friends are all gathered here for maintaining your health and for a specific healing process. You ask Him to assist you. He agrees. He then gets up and stands in front of you, holding His hands over and a short distance away from your head. You mentally count from one to three (allow time for the participants to count) and, with the count of three, you see a bright golden light emitted by your Master's hands. The light covers your entire body. Feel yourself completely immersed in this soft, beautiful, and peaceful bubble of golden light. Feel that this golden light is providing special energy for every cell, every tissue, every muscle, every bone, and every organ of your body. Feel that they are all perfectly healthy, functioning perfectly with respect to each other and with respect to the Universe. Feel yourself as being completely healthy. Feel your entire body rejuvenated and relaxed. If there is any part of your body needing any special healing attention, visualize this bright golden light as concentrated on that place, providing extra energy for its healing. See that place of your body as completely healed. Visualize and affirm that your. . . . (the place which needed special healing process) is now completely healed and you feel a special warmth in that location of your body. While your Master is still in front of you and you see your entire body as immersed in the bubble of golden light, you feel your entire body is healthy and you feel fine and very well. (Make sure you are not using any negative term or inducing any negativity. See the discussion of step (j) on page 137 in Chapter 10. Make a proper sentence, suitable for the healing process selected, for everyone to affirm mentally. Ask everyone to repeat that affirmation several times.)

(f) "Feel how wonderful it is to be completely healthy. Feel the place of your body that needed special healing attention as already being healed. You feel great there! Mentally affirm that you are very healthy and happy. (Repeat this last sentence several times.)

(g) "Now it is time to pay farewell to your Master and return your attention to this room. I will now count from one to nine, and with each count your attention and awareness will be directed more and more to this place. One . . . two . . . three. . . . (Count very slowly.) Your attention is now being directed to this room. Four . . . five . . . six. . . . You have left your mental Prashanti space and are returning to this place, feeling well and very happy, remembering everything that you have witnessed. Seven . . . eight. . . . With the count of nine, I would like you to open your eyes, feeling completely relaxed and happy, feeling well and joyous. Nine. Open your eyes, feeling very relaxed, serene and very, very happy."

7. After a moment or so of silence while everyone completely "returns" and opens his or her eyes, stop the music and ask if anyone would like to share his or her experience, and if anyone has any comment on the conduct of the relaxation, visualization, meditation, and linkage with his or her Master.

Group Visualization/Meditation
to Help Heal a Particular Person

This is similar to the activity discussed above, except that you visualize your Master standing in front of another person who needs healing instead of yourself. If the person can be present in the room, so much the better; otherwise, direct your attention to wherever he or she may be. Find out for sure what the problem with this person is in advance and which part of his or her body needs healing. Visualize your Master standing in front of him or her, radiating bright golden light to this person. Visualize that he or she is totally immersed in the bubble of golden light with its great healing power, with the radiation particularly concentrated on the part that needed special attention. See that part of his or her body as healed and that this person is completely healthy and happy.

Group Visualization/Meditation for Total Benefit

You can combine the linkage with a Master for health maintenance and healing process, or the one dealing with concentration of mind, or both of them, with the cultivation of human values, which was discussed as a group activity in Chapter 10.

The Role of Government in Health Maintenance

A major role of State and Federal governments is to invest in health maintenance and disease prevention for their citizens. The parable of the "cliff, fence, and ambulance" in Chapter 10 revealed that it is much wiser to build the fence around the cliff instead of enlarging the ambulance fleet. The role of governments is to do just that.

In this and the previous chapters, we discussed the power of mind in healing, health maintenance, and cultivation of human values. One role suggested for governments in the previous chapter was to establish centers for RICH-Values. With respect to health maintenance and healing, I would similarly like to propose the establishment of centers or institutes for:

Research Into the Utilization of the Power of Mind for Health Maintenance and Healing.

These centers can carry out the following tasks.

1. Explore the functioning and the power of mind.

2. Explore methods by which people can utilize their own power of mind to heal themselves and maintain good health.

3. Explore the effects of various food items, particularly meats and other animal products, on the functioning of the human mind. Knowledge exists on the effects of these products on the human body; it would be valuable to have such knowledge on the human mind.

4. Explore the effect of the well-being of the environment on the well-being and happiness of humans.

12

SUMMARY OF STEPS TO ACHIEVE HAPPINESS

The hands which serve are holier than the lips which pray.

—Sri Sathya Sai Baba

In this book, we have suggested ideas and presented procedures for acquiring happiness and sustainable joy. A part of attaining happiness is to love and respect nature and the environment, and to revere all beings on the planet. This calls for, among other things, developing modest lifestyles, placing ceilings on desires, conserving energy and other natural resources, and reducing environmental pollution. Such happiness is ever-lasting, the lifestyle sustainable, and the society joyous.

Here is a summary of the steps suggested in this book for attaining happiness, and for developing a sustainable, joyous society.

1. Accept that you live on this planet to be happy, and that there are joys in life which are much deeper than the sense pleasures.

2. Accept that you alone are responsible for your happiness. You can acquire happiness by developing a proper attitude and working hard to attain it.

3. Accept that deep happiness and joy can be secured through unconditional love and selfless service.

4. Depending on your interests and talents, find out what is the most effective and important service you can render, and do it. If you are planning a profession or a career, again based on your interests and abilities, find out the most effective service that you can render. Prepare for it whole-heartedly, and visualize yourself doing that service success-fully.

5. Accept that the Universe is abundant and very generous; that, through your own thoughts and efforts, the Universe will meet your needs; and that you do not need to expect anything from anyone. Never worry as to how you are going to make a living; trust that the Universe will provide.

6. In your service, never plan for wealth, fame, or the fruits of your action. Just serve unconditionally, with total love. If wealth and fame come because of your service, so be it; never become attached to them, and never become arro-gant. Use them to serve more.

7. Make use of all your knowledge and abilities to plan and execute anything that you need to accomplish, but accept the outcome, whatever it may be, and be content.

8. Think only of the good qualities of the people who occupy your mind. List these people's good qualities, so that any time their shortcomings come to your mind, you can refer to this list and see the goodness in them. Wish well for anyone and anything you see or think about.

9. Identify someone who symbolizes love and all the other positive human qualities, someone who has done selfless service, and someone whom you can easily love and relate to. I call this person a Master Teacher or, simply, a Master. This Master may be a living person or someone who has

lived in the past. Learn as much as you can about this Master. Any time your mind wanders around, direct it back to Him or Her. Keep the thought of this Master always in mind.

10. Develop a sense of reverence and respect for all beings, and never intentionally harm anyone or anything, including the environment. Accept a modest lifestyle, use as little as possible, and reuse or recycle as much as possible.

Using the parable of the bird flying on the wings of Love and Service, I can express the following as the essence of the steps for acquiring happiness:

(a) **Cultivate Love and the other human qualities through unconditional and selfless service.**

(b) **Identify a Master and keep the thought of Him or Her constantly in mind.**

MAY YOU ALWAYS
BE HAPPY

MAY ALL THE BEINGS IN THE WORLD
BE HAPPY

BIBLIOGRAPHY

1. David G. Myers, *The Pursuit of Happiness: Who Is Happy—and Why*, 1992, William Morrow and Co., Inc., New York.

2. Louise L. Hay, *Heal Your Body: The Mental Causes for Physical Illness and the Metaphysical Way to Overcome Them*, 1984, Hay House, Inc., Carson, California.

3. Mehdi N. Bahadori, *The University of Life*, 1993, Blue Dolphin Publishing, Inc., Nevada City, California.

4. Bernie S. Siegel, *Love, Medicine and Miracles*, 1986, Harper and Row, Publishers, New York.

5. Unknown Author, *Parable of the Dangerous Cliff*, Farm Review, May-June 1966, National Safety Council.

6. Loraine Burrows, Compiler, *Sathya Sai Education in Human Values*, 1988, Distributed by Sathya Sai Book Center of America, Tustin, California.

7. Vinayak K. Gokak, *On Sai Education: Human Values*, Sathya Sai Newsletter, Vol. 16, No. 4, Summer 1992, Distributed by Sathya Sai Book Center of America, Tustin, California.

8. Vinayak K. Gokak, *The First Four Years of Sri Sathya Sai Institute of Higher Learning*, 1987, Distributed by Sathya Sai Book Center of America, Tustin, California.

9. Norman V. Peale, *Seven Values to Live By*, 1992, Peale Center for Christian Living, Pawling, New York.

10. Tracy Deliman and John S. Smolowe, *Holistic Medicine: Harmony of Body, Mind and Spirit*, 1982, Reston Publishing Co., Inc., Reston, Virginia.

11. Steven Locke and Douglas Colligan, *The Healer Within: the New Medicine of Mind and Body*, 1986, E.P. Dutton, New York.

12. Deepak Chopra, *Quantum Healing: Exploring the Frontier of Mind/Body Medicine*, 1989, Bantam Books, New York.

13. Deepak Chopra, *Perfect Health: the Complete Mind/Body Guide*, 1991, Harmony Books, New York.

14. Elliott S. Dacher, *Psychoneuroimmunology (PNI): The New Mind/Body Healing Program*, 1991, Paragon House, New York. Quotations reprinted with permission of Paragon House Publications.

15. David Reuben, *The Save-Your-Life Diet: High-Fiber Protection from Six of the Most Serious Diseases of Civilization*, 1975, Random House, New York.

16. Andrew Weil, *Natural Health, Natural Medicine*, 1990, Houghton Mifflin Co., Boston.

MAY ALL THE BEINGS

IN THE WORLD

BE HAPPY

MEHDI N. BAHADORI

Scientific Background

Mehdi N. Bahadori received a
Ph.D. degree in mechanical engineering from the University of Illinois in
1964. He has a total of twenty-nine
years of teaching or research experience in five different countries, including the University of Missouri at
Rolla, Arizona State University in Tempe, California State University in Fullerton, in the United States, and University of
Waterloo in Waterloo, Canada. He has taught both graduate and
undergraduate courses in thermodynamics, energy conversion and
conservation, and research methods. He is a dynamic teacher and
lecturer who easily stimulates the students' interest in the subject
he teaches. He has always been liked and highly respected by his
students and colleagues.

Professor Bahadori has done pioneering research in the fields
of solar energy applications and passive cooling of buildings and
has published extensively in reputable journals, including *Scientific American*. He has six patents and has presented scientific
papers, chaired technical sessions, conducted workshops, and
lectured at many international and national conferences throughout the world. He has travelled to thirty-five countries of the world
in more than one hundred visits.

Spiritual Background

Dr. Bahadori has been interested in spiritual matters for the
past forty years. He has read extensively in this area and has
attended many spiritual seminars, lectures and gatherings. He has
been fortunate to visit Sri Sathya Sai Baba three times in India

and to receive His blessings each time. He has shared his experiences with this Master in many of the Sai Baba Centers in the United States and abroad.

Dr. Bahadori believes not only that there exists a purpose for creation, but that there is also a very delicate and precise order in the Universe. He believes that there is a reason for all that people experience in life. With his scientific and spiritual backgrounds, Professor Bahadori has developed a hypothesis that he calls THE UNIVERSITY OF LIFE (Blue Dolphin, 1993). He has had the opportunity to present this idea in a number of seminars throughout the country.

Also by Mehdi N. Bahadori: *The University of Life*

"Living on this planet is like going to a university, the University of Life. In this University everyone, irrespective of age, sex, color, and place of birth or residence, is both a student and a teacher, and all of Earth's natural resources are the University's supporting staff. The University of Life is established for us to learn important lessons. We learn that each of us is a unique and beautiful manifestation or face of God, and that each of us is playing a very important role in His very exciting drama of creation. Life's important lesson is to teach each person to recognize the self as one with everyone, with everything, and with God. One begins to consider everyone as one's brother or sister, and every plant, insect, and animal as one's cousin. In The University of Life one accepts every event as part of the learning process and every person in one's life as a teacher. . . "

ISBN 0-931892-70-8 96 pages $7.95